RealSmart
Baby Food™

How to Make 3-Months Worth of Delicious, Nutritious Baby Food in 3 One-Hour Blocks of Time

by Lisa Barrangou, Ph.D.

Bon Appétit!
Lisa

photography by Loan Rathgeber

RealFood Doctor Press
Raleigh, NC

RealSmart Baby Food™
www.RealSmartBabyFood.com

Published by RealFood Doctor Press
Raleigh, NC
Email: RealFoodDoc@gmail.com

First Edition
First printing, 2013

Printed in the United States of America

ISBN 978-0-9885887-0-7

Designed by Jessica Nordskog

Photography by Loan Rathgeber

Disclaimer: Although the author has made every effort to ensure that the information in this book was correct at press time, the author and publisher do not assume and hereby disclaim any liability to any party for any loss, damage, or disruption caused by errors or omissions, whether such errors or omissions result from negligence, accident, or any other cause. This book is not intended as a substitute for the medical advice of physicians. The reader should regularly consult a physician in matters relating to his/her health and the health of others.

Table of Contents

Bonus Chapters

Index

RealSmart
Baby Food™

www.RealSmartBabyFood.com

Acknowledgments

This book has been one of my favorite projects to have worked on, and it would not be all that it is without the help of some very talented, patient, and supportive people. Immense gratitude goes to Loan Rathgeber, for graciously offering her photography skills and bringing absolute beauty to this book. Your talent, time, advice and friendship are so greatly valued and appreciated. To my reviewers, Dr. Blair Guidera, Dr. Michelle Wong, and Jennifer Baldock (and a few others who would rather remain nameless), thank you for offering your time and individual expertise to enhance the content of this book. To Shannon Seip, thank you for offering an insider's perspective on the process of publishing a book, but most importantly, thank you for connecting me with Jessica Nordskog, my "design waitress," and the best designer I could have hoped to work with. Jessica, your artistic talent and style were paramount in bringing this book to life. Thank you for so patiently and kindly accepting my numerous revisions and requests. A personal thank you goes to my dear friend, Molly, for setting me on the path to "healthy living" decades ago, and always being there to remind me how to find my way. Gratitude must also be expressed to the countless mothers and friends whom I have had the privilege to know and share this wonderful experience of motherhood with. To those of you who said "You should write a book!", thank you. With your encouragement, I eventually did. Finally, to my husband, Rodolphe, for being my ever-present sounding board, reviewer and critic, and allowing me the freedom to run with this project. And last but not least, thank you to my three children, Benjamin, Emilie, and Patrick, for inspiring the content of this book and keeping me energized to always do more.

As a food professional who previously worked for three different Fortune 500 food companies, I have seen first hand what *processed food* truly is. What it is not is fresh, naturally nutrient-rich, naturally beautiful, flavorful, *real* food. When I had my first child I immediately knew that homemade baby food, made from whole, real foods, with no additives or fillers, would be my baby's food source when solid food feeding began. And so, my homemade baby food making journey began. I have been making baby food since 2005, for each of my three children, my friends' children, and for clients through my homemade baby food service company, *The Green Baby Chef™*.

I originally created my homemade baby food service for parents who value high-quality food for their baby, who want an alternative to overly processed, nutritionally inferior, void-of-taste jarred foods, but who don't have the time nor the energy to make it themselves. The appeal of this service was the creation of 3-months worth of wholesome, delicious baby food in a 3-hour timeframe, all safely made in the clients' kitchen, conveniently packaged and compactly stored in their freezer, taking up no more space than a small basket. While this service is valued by many, there are many more parents who truly want to make their baby's food themselves, which is a very rewarding experience. I have had many parents ask me for tips and recipes, hoping for me to share my "3-months in 3-hours" strategy. This book is my attempt to do just that.

I have developed a wonderfully efficient, flexible, comprehensive homemade baby food plan that is designed for you to implement at home. The food is smart and the strategy is smart. This plan includes every detail you need to create a well-balanced, diverse selection of whole food purées and freshly ground grains to feed your baby for up to 3 months, and to do it within 3 one-hour blocks of time. Rather than providing you with elaborate recipes, *RealSmart Baby Food™* guides you to prepare whole foods individually, using single ingredient recipes, and then shows you how to combine your individual creations for an endless number of flavorful, nutritionally balanced meal possibilities. In addition to recipes (which include helpful tips on how to select fresh whole foods), this comprehensive plan includes detailed shopping lists, guidelines for how to use each 1-hour block of time, a 3-month sample menu, in-depth nutritional information, and much more. The plan is flexible enough to take you through the various stages of your baby's palate development, and the information provided prepares you for knowing how to feed your baby wholesome foods for a lifetime.

My hope is that this book will help you with feeding your baby only the best that nature provides, while allowing you to accomplish that in an amazingly efficient amount of time. The recipes provided in this book are for foods that my babies started out eating, which are the same foods that they continue eating today, the only difference being that I don't have to purée them anymore. I firmly believe that if you start babies off with flavorful whole foods, they will know what real food is, and they will desire it as they grow.

From one parent to another,
Bon Appétit!

Creating a well-balanced, diverse offering of meals that baby will enjoy can be the most challenging part of feeding your baby. This challenge is largely responsible for why so many parents leave it up to food companies to create and supply baby's food for them. While commercially processed, jarred baby food does offer a convenience, homemade baby food made from fresh whole foods is far superior, both in nutrient and flavor quality. *Whole foods* are foods that are unprocessed and unrefined (or processed and refined as little as possible), and therefore maintain their natural flavor and nutrient integrity. Whole foods should be thought of as foods that can typically be found in nature (whole fruits, vegetables, unrefined grains, fresh cuts of meat, etc.). Jarred baby foods, while made mostly, but not entirely, from whole foods, are subject to very high temperature and pressure treatments, which is what allows them to remain shelf stable for literally years, but results in substantial nutrient and flavor loss. The impact of this high heat can be clearly seen by comparing the color of jarred peas with fresh or frozen peas (see below). The dramatic color change that results from excess heat is directly indicative of nutrient and flavor quality loss. In addition to extensive processing, jarred baby foods often include thickening agents such as flours, starches and gums, to increase stability (prevent them from separating during long term storage), effectively diluting the nutrient density of the product.

Jarred pea purée (left) vs. homemade pea purée (right).

Homemade baby food, on the other hand, made exclusively from fresh whole foods, can be prepared using gentle cooking methods, ensuring the maximum retention of nutrient and flavor integrity. Storing homemade baby food in the freezer is a gentle preservation method that locks in nutrients, rather than destroying them, allowing this nutrient and flavor integrity to carry over until consumption. When babies are offered gently processed, flavorful whole food purées, rather than overly processed jarred purées, they learn to accept and enjoy the natural, beautiful flavors that nature provides. This early acceptance, if cultivated, becomes a preference, and carries on with baby through life. Conversely, the bland flavors of jarred baby food purées often leads to an underdeveloped palate that is less accepting of the full flavors of healthy foods, and that too, can be carried on through life.

One of the underrated benefits of making homemade baby food is that it provides an opportunity for you, the primary food provider, to get more familiar with preparing whole foods, making it easier to offer these wholesome foods to your baby when they have moved beyond purées and onto a mature diet. Many parents who depend upon jarred purées to feed baby continue to look for processed food options as baby matures beyond purées, struggling to get into a routine of providing foods from natural sources. Researchers have found that consumption patterns for fruits and vegetables often change adversely as baby transitions from purées to a mature diet. A specific study[1] found that deep-yellow vegetables were consumed by 39% of babies at 7-8 months old, but only by 13% of babies at 19-24 months old, when French Fries became the most commonly consumed vegetable. They also found that at 19-24 months old, nearly one-third of babies consumed no fruit, while 60% consumed baked desserts, 20% candy, and 44% sweetened beverages on a given day. In our current western food culture where processed foods and fast foods are prevalent, many households have lost the skill of preparing whole foods in their own kitchen. Preparing homemade baby food is an opportunity to learn, or re-learn, that skill set, which is essential to providing healthy

1. Fox MK, Pac S, Devaney B, Jankowski L. Feeding infants and toddlers study: what foods are infants and toddlers eating? J Am Diet Assoc. 2004; 104 (1 suppl 1):s22-s30.

eating options for the entire family. And remember, as baby gets older and begins to have more power over the types of foods he will eat, the adage "do as I do" works much more effectively than "do as I say" at influencing his eating choices and preferences.

Preparing homemade baby food is actually very easy to do, but it does take time, the right cooking tools and a lot of planning to provide a diverse, well-balanced offering of age-appropriate food. *RealSmart Baby Food*™ was designed to do most of the necessary planning for you, guiding you through a 6-step process that will prepare you to make 3-months worth of baby food in just 3 one-hour blocks of time. After guiding you through the process of efficiently preparing a large supply of individual whole food purées, *RealSmart Baby Food*™ shows you how to combine your individual purées into an endless variation of flavorful, nutritionally balanced meals. Creating a well-balanced, diverse offering of meals that baby will enjoy may be the most challenging part of feeding your baby, but *RealSmart Baby Food*™ significantly alleviates that challenge by comprehensively guiding you through the entire process.

RealSmart Baby Food™ is organized into three sections. **Section 1** contains information you should consider before starting the homemade baby food process, including: feeding timelines and guidelines; specific health concerns to be aware of when feeding baby; and safe food preparation practices. **Section 2** contains *The RealSmart Strategy*™, the guide to creating 3-months worth of baby food in 3 one-hour blocks of time. **Section 3** contains individual purée recipes that will be used when implementing *The RealSmart Strategy*™, as well as detailed tips for selecting and preparing whole foods. This book is designed to be read continuously, but you may choose to jump to specific sections or chapters, depending upon your previous knowledge and experience in the kitchen.

Section 1

Before You Begin

Chapter 1
Feeding Timeline and Guidelines

When to Start

The American Academy of Pediatrics (AAP) and World Health Organization (WHO) currently recommend that solid food be introduced at around 6 months of age. Some pediatricians recommend starting solid foods during the age range of 4–6 months, while others will argue to be more stringent and wait out the full 6 months.

Note that introducing solid foods earlier than 4 months of age may interfere with baby's ability to consume adequate nutrients and calories due to prematurely displacing breast milk or formula, and may increase the risk of developing food allergies. On the other hand, delaying introduction of solid foods beyond the age of 6 months may lead to adverse consequences, including: decreased growth because baby may no longer obtain adequate calories from breast milk or formula alone; a resistance from baby to trying solid foods and an accompanying aversion to texture; and iron deficiency anemia.

In addition to the age milestone of around 6 months, infants should also be able to show the following:

- Sit upright with support.
- Have good head and neck control.
- Display readiness for varied textures by placing hands and/or toys in their mouth.
- Open mouth and lean forward when offered food; lean back and turn away when uninterested in food.
- Ability to swallow food when placed in their mouth instead of pushing it back out (Infants have an extrusion reflex, or thrust reflex, which causes them to raise the tongue and push against any object placed between their lips. This reflex usually disappears at 4–5 months of age).

Order of Introduction

The practice of introducing solid foods during the first year of life has varied over time and across cultures, and recommendations remain variable today. This variability exists because many feeding guidelines are based more on tradition and speculation than on scientific evidence. A wide range of advice is available, from which food categories should be offered and in which specific order (e.g. vegetables before fruits), to which order specific foods within a food category should be offered (e.g. sweet potatoes, then squash, then broccoli, etc.). In the U.S., cereals, fruits and vegetables are generally introduced first, followed by legumes, then dairy (yogurt, cheeses) and meats. Keep in mind that there are other cultures who introduce dairy or meat first. The point is that the order of introduction does not necessarily matter. Choose whichever order you and baby feel most comfortable with. The goal should be to gradually get baby to consume a diet filled with a wide variety of healthy whole foods.

One at a Time, Then Combine

Although the order of introduction is not necessarily important, it is advisable to introduce only one new food at a time in the effort to screen for allergies (see **Chapter 2**). It is typically recommended to offer an individual food for 3–5 days before introducing a new food. Once it has been determined that a food is well tolerated, feel free to combine it with other foods, including new foods. A sample 3-Month Menu of Meals displaying this approach is provided on pages 82-83.

Water and Juice

Once baby starts eating solids foods, start offering water as well. Give baby her own sippy cup filled with water and make it available during solid food feedings. Breast milk or formula will keep baby sufficiently hydrated, but baby should learn the skill of self-quenching thirst, and the age of 6 months is an appropriate time to start learning.

Juices should play a limited part in baby's diet. It is very easy for babies to consume a lot of juice because they readily accept sweet flavors. Although juices can be a source of many nutrients, it is much more beneficial to rely on consuming whole fruits for meeting nutrient needs. Whole fruits contain fiber (juices do not), which helps to control blood sugar response when digesting the natural sugars present in fruit. Juices can be consumed more rapidly than whole fruit, making the risk for over consumption greater. When given in excess, juices can contribute to significant sugar and calorie consumption. Juices should not be given at all prior to 6 months of age. When juices are given, they should be regarded as a treat rather than a staple of baby's diet. Be sure to provide sources that are labeled as 100% juice, instead of those sweetened with additional sugars.

Foods To Avoid

Honey and Corn Syrup: Honey and corn syrup may contain spores of *Clostridium botulinum*, which can cause botulism in infants because their digestive systems are not mature enough to prevent the growth of these spores. Honey and corn syrup may be introduced after 12 months of age.

Cow's Milk: Cow's milk should not be introduced before 12 months of age. Breast milk or formula should be the exclusive source of milk until this time. Other dairy products containing cow's milk (yogurt, cheeses) are fine in moderate quantities. Cow's milk, in particular, contains high amounts of some specific proteins and fats that are difficult for infants to digest and absorb. The amounts of these hard-to-digest components of milk are significantly decreased during the process of culturing yogurts and cheeses.

Raw-Milk Cheeses: Raw-milk cheeses are made from unpasteurized milk, which may contain very harmful pathogens (*E. coli* O157:H7, *Listeria*, *Salmonella*), particularly for infants and children. Completely avoid raw-milk cheeses until at least the age of 5 years.

High-Acid Fruits: Citrus fruits, tomatoes, pineapple, and strawberries are highly acidic fruits that can cause food sensitivities for some infants.

One common symptom is a severe diaper rash. Baby is typically better able to digest these fruits after 12 months of age.

High Nitrate Vegetables: Infants younger than 6 months of age do not have a mature enough digestive system to properly digest nitrates. Vegetables naturally found to have high nitrate content include root vegetables (beets, carrots), green beans and leafy greens (spinach, kale, chard). These vegetables are safe to consume after 6 months of age. See page 174 for more details.

High Mercury Fish: Infants and young children are advised to entirely avoid fish containing high levels of mercury, which can harm their developing nervous systems. High level mercury fish include: shark, swordfish, tilefish, king mackerel, ahi and bigeye tuna, orange roughy, and marlin. Completely avoid high mercury fish until at least the age of 5 years. See page 176 for more details.

How Much

For the first year of life, breast milk or formula should continue to be baby's primary source of nutrition. Baby will start out eating as little as 1–2 tablespoons of solid food at a time. Initially baby should eat solid food only once per day, as eating is only for practice at this point, instead of for nutrition. Solid food should be given after, not before, an offering of breast milk or formula, so as not to result in disinterest in milk. When baby starts to seem hungrier more often, or not satisfied after a breast milk or formula feeding, begin to gradually increase the frequency of solid food feedings and the amount offered at each meal. Breast milk or formula feedings will naturally decline as solid foods become increasingly more important. *Every baby is different, so there is no one correct amount or strict advice to give regarding quantity of solid foods or the rate of breast milk or formula decline.* You decide what baby will eat, but let baby decide whether or not to eat and how much to eat. Follow baby's cues. Never force baby to finish a meal. Infants and young children know how to self-regulate eating much better than most adults. We tend to lose that skill as we get older, though there is no reason why we should. By the time baby is 12 months old, he should be eating 3 solid meals per day, with an additional 1–2 snacks.

Flavor and Texture, Color and Nutrients (FaT CaN)

There are four key food attributes to keep in mind as you begin the adventure of feeding baby solid foods: **F**lavor and **T**exture, **C**olor and **N**utrients (*FaT CaN*). To remember *FaT CaN*, think of *"fat can be healthy,"* which is discussed below. If baby's meals are *flavorful*, with the appropriate *texture*, and if you are offering whole foods from every *color* of the rainbow, while keeping *nutrients* in mind, you will provide consistently well balanced meals that will please baby's palate and nourish her body.

Flavor

Obviously, flavor is an important part of the eating experience. If baby does not like the flavor of something, it will likely be rejected. Whole foods are bursting with their own unique and beautiful flavors. Baby may not like all flavors when initially introduced to them, but do not let that discourage you. New foods may need to be introduced repeatedly, maybe as many as 10 times, for acceptability to develop. And remember, if baby is given the full opportunity to develop a taste for fresh fruits and vegetables, these preferences will follow him through life. These initial months of solid food introduction are the prime time for baby's palate to develop, and baby can quickly learn to become an adventurous eater. Studies have shown that lifetime flavor preferences are established by the age of 3 years. Seize this opportunity to introduce a wide variety of flavors. You should not assume or prematurely conclude that baby will only be interested in bland foods. In fact, breastfed babies have already been exposed to a wide array of flavors through breast milk, all directly influenced by mother's diet (an under-appreciated benefit of breastfeeding). Garlic and broccoli, both relatively strongly flavored foods, were/are loved by all three of my children, probably in part because I ate a ton of these foods while breastfeeding.

When the solid food eating experience begins, baby will initially be introduced to single whole foods (e.g. apples, peaches, green beans, etc.). As eating progresses, these flavorful individual whole foods can then be combined to provide more flavor depth, in addition to producing a more nutritionally balanced meal. Whole foods can also be strategically paired to mellow out particularly strong flavors that baby does not show acceptance to (e.g. pairing bananas with broccoli will allow the natural sweetness of bananas to detract from broccoli's strong, sulfurous flavor profile). The *Flavor Compatibility Charts* in **Chapter 5** will show you which whole foods have flavors that combine well, simplifying your job of creating flavorful meals for baby.

If desired, you can even begin to mildly season purées with some herbs and spices. Baby is going to eventually be eating the same table food as you, so it would be highly convenient if she found the seasonings you typically use in cooking to be acceptable. If you choose to introduce seasonings, start with very small quantities (just a pinch), and always taste food before offering to baby. Cinnamon and nutmeg are usually well received flavors. You could also try even bolder flavors such as curry spices, oregano, ginger, or any other seasonings you enjoy cooking with. Herbs and spices are fine additions to your baby's meal, but remember to avoid addition of salt or sugar. Babies have a natural affinity and preference for sugar, and if given access, will very quickly begin rejecting sugar-void foods. Salt added to baby's food causes unnecessary strain on her little developing kidneys, and also unnecessarily builds her palate's tolerance for salt as she grows.

Texture

As important as flavor is, controlling texture is even more important during the initial phases of introducing solid foods. If the texture is too thick or lumpy, no matter how flavorful the food is, baby will likely immediately reject it. Initial solid foods should have a very thin, liquid-like consistency. As baby learns to incorporate a chewing motion, he can progress to thicker, chunkier foods. Babies will vary widely on their readiness for texture changes. Typically by 7–8 months of age, baby is ready for some lumpiness or chunkiness.

It is relatively easy to manipulate texture if it needs changing. If a purée is made too thick, it can be thinned out with water, breast milk or formula. If it is too chunky, it will need to be puréed further. Conversely, if a purée is made too thin, it can easily be thickened with cereals (ground grains), plain yogurt, or paired with a thicker food. When baby is ready for thicker, chunkier foods, thin purées can be mixed with whole grains (oatmeal, couscous, quinoa, pasta, etc.), lentils, split peas, cottage cheese, plain yogurt, tiny pieces of meat, or many other combinations that result in a thicker, chunkier meal.

Remember to encourage progressive textures throughout the developing eating experience. If you wait too long to gradually move from ultra smooth purées up to chunky foods, baby may develop a texture aversion that will be challenging to outgrow.

Color

The colors of whole foods typically reflect the different *phytonutrients* they contain, such as carotenoids (orange carrots), anthocyanins (deep blue blueberries), lycopene (red tomatoes and watermelon), etc.. Unlike *nutrients* (see section below), phytonutrients are not considered essential to human life, but they are known to have a significant role in positively impacting human health. Phytonutrients (also called phytochemicals) are organic components of plants that are thought to promote human health through a variety of functions, including acting as antioxidants, enhancing immune response, repairing DNA damage, causing cancer cells to die (apoptosis), detoxifying carcinogens, and more. Phytonutrients are particularly effective antioxidants, functioning to quench *free radicals* that are encountered in the environment and during the digestion of some foods. (The build up of free radicals in the body over time is predominantly responsible for the aging process.)

There are many different types of phytonutrients, with some of the most commonly discussed in foods including carotenoids, phenols, polyphenols, anthocyanins, flavones, isoflavones, terpenes, phytosterols, and many more. Many phytonutrients are directly related to plant colors. Generally, the brighter and bolder the colors, the more concentrated the phytonutrients. Since each phytonutrient provides unique beneficial functions to the human body, a well balanced diet should include as many phytonutrients, or colors, as possible. *Offer baby whole foods from every color of the rainbow.*

Nutrients

For the first year of life, breast milk or formula should continue to be baby's primary source of nutrition. Solid foods will incrementally take a larger place in baby's diet, and as she approaches her first birthday it will become very important to understand how to meet her nutritional needs through predominantely solid foods. While the ability to effectively manage baby's nutrient intake requires some understanding of specific nutrients and their food sources, meticulously calculating amounts of individual nutrients consumed is not necessary (unless advised by your pediatrician to do so, due to specific health concerns). Follow the simple guidelines below to feed baby a nutrient-rich, balanced diet.

✱ GOOD TO KNOW

Phytonutrients form part of the immune system of plants and function to protect them from diseases, injuries, insects, pollutants, drought, excessive heat and ultraviolet rays. Since organic plants have to fight harder than conventional (non-organic) plants to protect themselves from these environmental stresses (because they have not been treated with commercial pesticides and other chemicals to "protect" them), organic plants typically have higher concentrations of phytonutrients.

Offer whole foods: nature provides everything baby needs

Baby's diet should be mainly composed of a wide variety of *whole foods* (foods that are unprocessed and unrefined, or processed and refined as little as possible), including the categories of fruits, vegetables, legumes, nuts, seeds, whole grains, meats, fish, dairy and eggs. Whole foods each contain their own unique supply of naturally abundant nutrients. Consuming a wide array of whole foods, including a variety of whole food categories and variety within each category, will ensure nutrient needs are being met. Dietary supplements and fortified products are rarely needed when a diverse selection of whole foods form the foundation of a healthy diet.

Limit processed foods

Processed foods are basically anything other than whole foods (see above). Processed foods usually come in packages layered with cardboard, foil and plastic, and are made with a long list of chemically deconstructed ingredients that are difficult to pronounce. Many of the ingredients used are not ideal or appropriate for baby's body to digest. Many processed foods (even organic versions) marketed as "kid" foods, snacks and drinks tend to be high in refined sugars and are generally nutrient-poor. Since they displace natural whole foods in baby's diet, processed foods should be limited.

Do not restrict dietary fat and calories during the first 2 years of life

Fats are an especially important source of calories and nutrients for infants and toddlers. Their rapidly growing bodies and developing brains during the early months and years of life require the dense calories and structural and chemical properties that fats provide. Remember: *FaT CaN be healthy!* This is specifically true when fat is obtained from natural sources (whole foods), and is consumed as part of a balanced diet.

Pay attention to protein

In addition to being an essential macronutrient for many of the body's functions and development, adequate intake of protein will help to keep baby's blood sugar levels regulated, and result in increased satiety and sustained energy. Aim to incorporate some form of protein at every meal.

Pay attention to iron

Baby's natural iron stores are typically depleted by 6 months of age, and iron must be adequately consumed from solid foods to avoid iron-deficiency anemia, the most common nutritional deficiency among infants. It is important to note that iron from meat sources is much more readily absorbed than iron from plant sources. When relying on plant sources of iron, pairing the iron source with a vitamin C-rich food will greatly enhance iron absorption when consumed together at the same meal.

Pay attention to calcium

When breast milk or formula consumption significantly declines, usually by baby's first birthday, food sources of calcium should be included in his diet to ensure optimal development of bones and teeth, as well as for muscle, heart and digestive health.

	Protein	Iron	Calcium	Vitamin C
Fruits		√ *(dried fruits, especially apricot)*	√ *(dried fruits)*	√ *(especially berries, citrus, mangoes, papaya, kiwi, cantaloupe)*
Vegetables		√ *(leafy greens, potatoes w/skins, asparagus)*	√ *(leafy greens, broccoli)*	√ *(especially leafy greens, broccoli, cauliflower, turnips)*
Legumes	√	√	√ *(edamame, garbanzo beans)*	
Nuts	√	√	√	
Seeds	√	√ *(especially sesame (tahini))*	√ *(especially sesame (tahini))*	
Whole Grains	√	√ *(quinoa, barley, wheat)*		
Dairy	√		√	
Eggs	√	√	√	
Meat/Fish	√	√		

Important nutrients to monitor for baby, and their main food sources. *Italicized foods* indicate specific foods within the given food category known to supply the nutrient. This chart was compiled through analyzing data of individual whole foods using the USDA National Nutrient Database.

> **✳ Tip**
>
> Refer to **Bonus Chapter 1** (page 158) for additional nutrition information, including a detailed discussion of specific nutrients and their food sources (and a more thorough nutrient chart on page 173).

Timeline and Milestones for Feeding Baby

| 1mo | 2mo | 3mo | 4mo | 5mo | 6mo | 7mo | 8mo | 9mo | 10mo | 11mo | 12mo | 2yr | 5yr |

0-5 yrs

Choking is a significant hazard, take precautions | Avoide high mercury fish | Avoid raw milk cheeses

0-2 yrs

Do not restrict dietary fat or calories: *FaT CaN* be healthy!

0-12mo

Breast milk/formula is baby's primary nutrition source

0-6mo

Avoid nitrates (untested well water and high nitrate foods)

0-4mo

Exclusively feed baby breast milk/formula

6mo

Introduce solid foods (and water) | Baby's iron stores are depleted

7-8mo

Typical readiness for lumpy/chunky texture

9-11mo

Pincer grasp develops; introduce finger foods

10-12mo

Safe to introduce:
- Edible skins of fruits and veggies
- Gluten-containing grains

12mo

- Baby eating 3 solid meals per day & 1-2 snacks
- Safe to introduce:
  - cow's milk
  - honey/corn syrup
  - highly acidic fruits

Chapter 2
Health Concerns When Feeding Baby

Choking

Baby has a very small airway, and care must be taken to minimize risks of choking. Choking is a common cause of death in children under age one, and the danger remains significant until the age of five.

- Always supervise eating to be available to assist if baby begins choking.

- Keep baby seated and do not allow lying down, walking, running or playing while eating.

- Teach baby to take small bites and to chew completely.

- Finger foods should be cut no larger than 1/4 inch (6 mm). Small, circular foods, such as grapes should be quartered, blueberries should be halved, etc.

- Nuts can be a choking hazard. If allergies are not a concern (see *Allergies* section later in this chapter), nuts can safely be given to baby if they are finely ground in a food processor, blender or coffee grinder.

- Sticky foods such as peanut butter or other nut butters can be a choking hazard. Spread peanut butter or nut butters very thinly on toast or crackers.

Coughing is a natural response for trying to dislodge something stuck in the throat. If baby is coughing, allow him and encourage him to do so in order to dislodge the object. Do not try to remove a foreign object unless you can actually see it, or you could push it farther into the airway. If baby is making no sounds and appears not to be breathing, he is truly choking and you will need to assist.

It is advisable to set aside the time to take an infant and child CPR course to learn how to properly assist with choking and other potential health situations. To find a class in your area, visit the American Red Cross website (www.redcross.org) or call 800-RED-CROSS (800-733-2767).

Allergies and Food Intolerances

Allergies

When baby begins eating solid foods it is important to introduce individual foods one at at time in order to screen for food allergies. New foods should be offered for 3–5 days (which is how long it could take for an allergic reaction to appear) before introducing another new food. Once it has been determined that a food is well tolerated, feel free to combine it with other foods, including new foods. Just be sure to introduce only one new food at a time, otherwise it will be very difficult to determine the source of any potential allergy.

According to the American Academy of Allergy, Asthma and Immunology, approximately 8% of children will develop a food allergy. Infants are at greatest risk for developing food allergies if they already have an atopic disease (asthma, eczema), or if one or both parents or a sibling has allergies or other atopic disease. A food allergy causes an immune system reaction that affects numerous organs in the body. In most cases, food allergies are mild, but in rare cases they can be severe, sometimes triggering life-threatening conditions. If a food allergy is present, even a tiny amount of the offending food can cause an immediate reaction.

Many different foods can trigger an allergic reaction, but the following 8 foods or groups of foods are responsible 90% of the time:

- **Peanuts**
- **Cow's Milk**
- **Shellfish**
- **Soy**
- **Fish**
- **Eggs**
- **Wheat**
- **Tree Nuts**

Common signs of an allergic reaction include, but are not limited to:

- **Hives**
- **Rash**
- **Difficulty breathing**
- **Face, tongue or lip swelling**
- **Wheezing**
- **Vomiting**
- **Diarrhea**
- **Gassiness**

It has been previously recommended that parents delay or avoid feeding infants and young children some of these highly allergenic foods to help prevent the possible development of food allergies. The American Academy of Pediatrics (AAP) revised its guidelines in 2008, however, after finding that *there is no convincing evidence that avoiding these foods during the early months and years will prevent food allergies.* The AAP no longer recommends avoiding highly allergenic foods, unless baby is at high risk for allergy development (baby already suffers from another atopic disease, or has a sibling or parent with allergies or other atopic disease). Discuss this issue with your pediatrician if you have specific allergy concerns.

Food Intolerances

Food reactions (sensitivities) are common, but most are caused by *food intolerances* rather than food allergies. Symptoms of food intolerances vary greatly, and can sometimes be mistaken for symptoms of a food allergy. Food intolerance symptoms do not involve an immune system reaction and generally come on gradually. With a food intolerance, it is possible that small amounts of the offending food may be consumed without causing symptoms. With a true food allergy, however, a very tiny amount of the offending food will *always* trigger an immune response.

Many foods can cause food intolerances. Common food intolerances include lactose intolerance, gluten intolerance, sensitivity to food additives (including preservatives, colorings, flavorings, sulfites). Many infants display food intolerances for specific foods due to their immature digestive systems, but then outgrow these food intolerances sometime between their first and second birthdays.

> *If you suspect symptoms of a food allergy or intolerance, stop offering the suspected food and consult with your pediatrician. If baby is having trouble breathing, has swelling on the face, or develops severe vomiting or diarrhea after eating, call 911 immediately. Severe allergic reactions can be fatal very quickly.*

Vegetarian, Vegan, and Gluten-Free Diets

Vegetarian and Vegan

Feeding vegetarian and vegan diets to infants and toddlers can be a healthy lifestyle choice, *if* there is sufficient and adequate planning and attention to ensuring that all essential nutrients for proper growth are obtained in the diet. With proper planning, it is relatively easy to obtain an adequate supply of nutrients from a well-balanced vegetarian diet which includes dairy and eggs (lacto-ovo-vegetarian diet). It can be significantly more challenging, however, to ensure that an adequate supply of essential nutrients is obtained through a vegan diet, which strictly avoids any consumption of animal or animal-derived products. Vegan diets, especially for infants and young children, should be decided with great caution, and only with proper education and planning. Refer to **Bonus Chapter 1** and the nutrient chart on page 173 for helpful nutrient information.

Gluten-Free

A gluten-free diet is a diet that excludes the protein gluten. Gluten is found in several grains, including wheat, barley, rye and triticale (a cross between wheat and rye). A gluten-free diet is used to treat a spectrum of gluten intolerance disorders, ranging from mild gluten sensitivity to celiac disease, an autoimmune disorder characterized by a severe gluten sensitivity.

When gluten is consumed by people with celiac disease, it causes inflammation and gradually damages the wall of the small intestine, leading to poor absorption of vital nutrients and resulting in potential long-term health complications. Any form of gluten intolerance can cause dramatic intestinal distress (stomachaches, gas, diarrhea) and/or trigger additional health problems, including headaches, fatigue, joint or muscle pain, skin rashes, acne, or other symptoms.

Gluten intolerance can appear at any age, and since it can manifest itself in many different ways, it is often under-diagnosed or misdiagnosed. Celiac disease (the most severe form of gluten intolerance) can be definitively diagnosed by a physician using a two-step process: (1) testing the blood for antibodies activated by gluten, and, if antibodies are present, (2) a biopsy to look for intestinal damage. Gluten sensitivity, on the other hand, has a diagnosis by default. If a patient tests negative for celiac disease but sees improvement or eradication of symptoms after starting a gluten-free diet, they are determined to be gluten sensitive.

A gluten-free diet should always avoid wheat, barley, rye, and triticale. Common wheat variations to also look out for and avoid include bulgur, semolina, farina, Kamut®, graham flour, durum flour, and spelt. Oats can be contaminated with wheat during growing and processing, and should also be avoided unless specifically labeled and certified as gluten-free.

Grains Containing Gluten
Wheat (including bulgur, semolina, farina, Kamut®, graham, durum, spelt)
Barley
Rye
Triticale
Oats (if not certified gluten-free)

Many grains, starches and flours can be part of a gluten-free diet, and include: amaranth, arrowroot, buckwheat (don't let the name confuse you; it does *not* contain wheat), corn, flax, millet, quinoa, rice, sorghum, soy, tapioca, teff, potato flour, and bean flours.

Gluten-Free Grains, Starches and Flours	
Amaranth	Sorghum
Arrowroot	Soy
Buckwheat	Tapioca
Corn (polenta)	Teff
Flax	Potato Flour
Millet	Bean Flours
Quinoa	Oats (if certified
Rice	gluten-free)

A gluten-free diet may have a limited selection of grains, but many healthy, nutritious and delicious foods are naturally gluten-free, including fruits, vegetables, beans, nuts, seeds, eggs, meats, poultry, fish, and most dairy products. It is important, however, to make sure that these natural whole foods are not processed or mixed with gluten-containing grains, additives or preservatives when trying to maintain a gluten-free diet.

 Tip

Although any grain can be used for baby food, gluten-containing grains should be reserved for a later stage (around 10 months old) because they are more difficult to digest.

Digestive Health

Diarrhea

There are many potential causes for diarrhea in infants and young children. Always seek the advice of a pediatrician for treatment.

A commonly recommended dietary treatment for diarrhea is the BRAT diet. BRAT stands for Bananas, Rice, Applesauce, and Toast. Offer these foods to help firm up loose stools.

A specific treatment for diarrhea to consider and discuss with your pediatrician is offering *probiotics*. Probiotics are "good" bacteria that reside in the intestines and play an active role in maintaining digestive health. If a bacterial infection (from "bad" bacteria) is or was present, consuming probiotics can help restore balance to the digestive system, and effectively relieve diarrhea. It is also helpful to give probiotics following treatment with antibiotics, which, while taken to combat infectious bacteria, inadvertently destroy good bacteria residing in the intestines. Foods labeled as containing "live and active cultures," such as many yogurts, already contain probiotics. Probiotics can also be purchased as a dietary supplement, and can be mixed with baby's food.

Constipation

The digestive system takes time to learn how to process and absorb new nutrients, and one of the most common causes of constipation in infants is the introduction of solid foods.

To help relieve constipation, reverse the BRAT diet, and avoid bananas, rice, applesauce and toast. Natural foods to include in the diet that are effective at relieving constipation (acting as natural laxatives) include dried plums (prunes), mangoes, pears and apricots. Other techniques to help relieve constipation include giving baby a gentle tummy massage and moving her legs as if riding a bicycle, both of which promote digestive movement.

Gas

Gas is typically caused by either swallowed air (which can occur during lengthy bouts of crying) or from the normal breakdown of undigested foods. Foods that make their way to the large intestine undigested can be feasted upon by the friendly bacteria who live there. The result from bacteria eating undigested food is often gas.

Some foods, such as beans and cruciferous vegetables (broccoli, cabbage, etc.) contain oligosaccharides, which are specific carbohydrates (a form of fiber) that the human body does not have the enzymes to digest. When consumed, these oligosaccharides make their way to the large intestine undigested, and specific bacteria that reside there begin digesting them for you, occasionally producing gas in the process. You should not automatically assume that baby will have a difficult time digesting foods commonly known to produce gas. The types and quantities of intestinal bacteria vary among all people, resulting in some individuals experiencing very little gas while others have a lot of gas when oligosaccharides (or other types of fiber) are consumed. Additionally, many people will notice a gradual digestive improvement (decreased gas) when oligosaccharide-containing foods are gradually and continually introduced into the diet over a long period of time, as a kind of digestive tolerance develops.

Potentially gas-producing foods should not be feared. Many of these foods are loaded with nutritional benefits that should be taken advantage of. Gas is an entirely normal part of digestion and should really only be considered an issue if causing physical discomfort. If baby seems only slightly and temporarily uncomfortable when passing gas, there should be no cause for concern. If baby is noticeably uncomfortable, often turning red and crying while trying to pass gas, however, known gas-producing foods should be avoided (though they should be re-introduced later).

There are ways to reduce the occurrence of gas when consuming known gas-producing foods. Always gradually introduce known gas-producing foods into the diet to allow the digestive system time to adapt. Beans should be soaked and rinsed before cooking, which allows many of the water soluble oligosaccharides to come out of the beans and into the water. Cooking beans with *kombu*, a sea vegetable, is also known to improve digestion of beans by breaking down oligosaccharides during cooking (see page 149).

Chapter 3
Safe Food Preparation Practices

Keeping Things Clean

Clean hands, a clean kitchen and clean food are all necessary to avoid microbial contamination and potential illness from consuming foods.

- **Keep hands clean:** Wash hands thoroughly in warm soapy water for at least 20 seconds before preparing any food.

- **Keep working surfaces (cutting boards, counter tops), utensils and other cooking tools clean:** Use warm soapy water for cleaning. For sanitizing, use the dishwasher or 1 tablespoon of unscented, chlorinated bleach in 1 gallon of water.

- **Prevent cross-contamination:** Cross-contamination is the transfer of harmful bacteria to a food from another source, such as contaminated hands, cutting boards, utensils, surfaces, or other foods. Raw meats (which potentially contain pathogenic bacteria) and their juices should always remain separate from other foods, starting from the place of purchase all the way to the kitchen, remembering that meat juices can leak. Separate cutting boards should be designated for produce and raw meats to avoid cross-contamination.

- **Wash all fruits and vegetables:** Before preparation or eating, all fruits and vegetables should be washed under cold running tap water to remove any lingering dirt, and to reduce any microbial contamination that may be present. Do not wash produce with detergent or soap, which are not approved for use on food. Remember to wash the outside of all fruits and vegetables, including rind or skin that you plan to remove, to avoid pushing contaminated dirt into the produce with the knife when cutting. It is also necessary to wash pre-packaged frozen produce, which is typically not washed prior to packaging.

Storing Food

When you are finished preparing baby food purées, store them in the freezer or refrigerator within 2 hours. Food stored in the freezer constantly at 0° F or below will be safe indefinitely because no bacteria can grow at these cold temperatures. It is important to know that although freezing will prevent the growth of bacteria, it will not kill bacteria already present, so preventing potential contamination of food before freezing is necessary. Although bacteria will not grow at freezer temperatures, lengthy freezer storage may diminish the quality of the food. Long term freezer storage can result in freezer burn (when cold, dry freezer air pulls moisture out of food), resulting in a loss of texture and flavor, and absorption of other flavors from adjacent freezer foods. Freezer burn of frozen purée cubes can be minimized by removing as much air as possible from freezer storage bags. The quality of most frozen purée cubes can be maintained for at least 3 months. Fresh or thawed baby purées can safely be stored in the refrigerator for 3–5 days.

It is important to verify the temperature of your freezer and refrigerator. Your built-in temperature control dials may not be effective or calibrated correctly, so it is advisable to use a separate appliance thermometer to check the internal temperatures of your refrigerator and freezer. Your refrigerator should consistently be maintained at 40° F or below, and your freezer should be maintained at 0° F or below.

Thawing Food

The safest method for thawing frozen food is in the refrigerator. Most frozen purée cubes will thaw overnight (within 12 hours) when placed in the refrigerator. For a quick-thaw approach, frozen purée cubes can also be thawed directly on the stove top in a small pot over low heat. A microwave may be used to thaw frozen purée cubes, though the use of microwaves is a controversial subject matter that I do not personally recommend. There are many studies indicating the use of microwaves may pose both potential health dangers and excessive nutrient loss from foods. If you do choose to use a microwave, consider using glass instead of plastic containers for re-heating frozen purée cubes, and take care to avoid hot-spots by stirring food very well before serving to baby.

It is not advisable to thaw food at room temperature because bacteria, if present, can multiply rapidly. Freezing can keep food safe indefinitely, however once food begins to thaw and become warmer than 40° F, any bacteria that may have been present before freezing can begin to multiply. The "danger zone" for bacterial growth is 40–140° F (5–58° C), and food should not be left in this danger zone for greater than 2 hours. Once frozen purée cubes have safely thawed, they can be stored in the refrigerator for 3–5 days. Do not refreeze thawed baby food purées.

Cooking Meats

If preparing meats for baby (see page 64), it is necessary to ensure that all meats are thoroughly cooked. To determine doneness, insert a food thermometer into the thickest part of the food, making sure it does not touch bone, fat or gristle. Cook food until the thermometer reads at least the internal temperature listed below. Clean the thermometer with hot, soapy water before and after each use.

Meat	Internal Temperature
All poultry (chicken, turkey, etc.)	165° F (74° C)
Ground beef, pork or egg dishes	160° F (71° C)
Beef, veal or lamb steaks and roasts	145° F (63° C)
Fish	145° F (63° C)

Heating Food

If prepared baby food contains meat, fish, dairy products or eggs, it is necessary to reheat the food to 165° F and then let the food cool down to a luke warm temperature before feeding to baby. The frozen purée cubes created from the *RealSmart Recipes*™ in this book (which do not contain meat, fish, dairy products or eggs) do not need to be heated after thawing, and can be consumed at a cool or room temperature as desired.

Left-Overs

If baby has finished eating and there is food left over, it is advisable to throw away any remaining food from the container baby was eating from. Germs from baby's mouth will be introduced into the container from the spoon used to feed baby, and these germs will subsequently grow in the food during storage. To avoid wasting a lot of baby food, spoon out small portions from the food container into another feeding bowl. The uneaten food in the food container that has not been contaminated from baby's spoon can then be stored again in the refrigerator.

Section 2

·········· The RealSmart Strategy™ ··········

Chapter 4

3-MONTHS IN 3-HOURS

The RealSmart Strategy™ will guide you through each of the following 6 steps to create 3-months worth of wholesome, delicious, nutritious baby food in 3 one-hour blocks of time:

1. **Selecting a Menu of Whole Foods**
2. **Preparing a Shopping List**
3. **Creating Space**
4. **Shopping**
5. **Creating a Mise en Place Plan**
6. **Cooking Sessions**

Steps 1–5 will prepare you for your three cooking sessions (*Step 6*), which is where you will spend your 3 one-hour blocks of time. Each of your cooking sessions will be spent preparing one-third of the 3-month baby food supply. These three different time blocks, each separated by at least 1 day, are necessary to minimize equipment needs and freezer space during the initial freezing process. After all three cooking sessions have been completed, you will have 3-months worth of baby food made, compactly stored, and be ready to start feeding baby.

> *The RealSmart Strategy*™ is designed as a flexible plan allowing you to build a custom baby food supply using whole foods of your choice. To further simplify this plan, you have the option to use a sample *menu of whole foods* and accompanying tools (*shopping list* and *mise en place plan*) described in the following sections, instead of creating your own.

The RealSmart Strategy™
will show you how to turn this:

Starting Ingredients:
Actual ingredients for a 3-month supply of baby food, based on the *RealSmart Whole Foods Menu.*

Into this:

Final Product:
Actual 3-month supply of baby food, as frozen purée cubes, conveniently packaged, organized, and compactly stored in your freezer.

There are a few basic tools that you will need to have on hand for preparing and storing homemade baby food. Anything you may need to purchase can be used in your kitchen well beyond the years of making baby food, as these tools are not baby food specific.

Many of the kitchen tools mentioned below are available at
www.RealSmartBabyFood.com

Blender or food processor: Most blenders and food processors will get the job done for making baby food. High-speed blenders, however, have a much more powerful motor than regular blenders or food processors, and can produce an ultra smooth purée like no other machine can. For the king of all blenders, I highly recommend the Vitamix®, which is solid, powerful, reliable, and durable. In addition to producing ultra smooth purées, the Vitamix® can also produce perfectly ground grains for baby cereals, and can handle tough jobs, such as creating nut butters. This quality machine is rather expensive, but it is one of the best kitchen investments you can ever make if you commit to a healthy lifestyle of eating whole foods, beyond the homemade baby food making years.

Steamer: This tool is essential for preparing baby food using *steamer recipes* in this book. There are many different types of steamers to choose from, including single or multi-layered steamer pots, individual metal or silicone steamer baskets that can sit inside of a standard pot, bamboo

Silicone Steamer Basket

steamers, and countertop electric steamers with multi-layered steamer baskets. My favorite steamers are multi-layered steamers (since you can cook multiple foods at one time), and individual silicone baskets that sit inside of a standard pot (see photo on page 42). I like these silicone steamers because the flexibility of their material allows them to fit into different sized pots and also allows easy transfer of steamed foods directly into the blender. Only one steamer basket is necessary to use *The RealSmart Strategy™,* but multiple steamers will make you even more efficient. Whichever steamer you choose, the diameter of the basket should be at least 11 inches to accommodate the recipe sizes in this book.

Small pot with lid: Needed for *heat/steep recipes* in this book.

Colander: Needed for rinsing and draining whole foods.

Cutting board: Needed for cutting and preparing whole foods.

Knife: Needed for cutting whole foods. Use any well-sharpened knife of your choice, remembering that more accidents happen with dull knives than sharp knives.

Vegetable peeler: Used for peeling skins off of whole foods.

Prep bowls (6): Used for holding and separating individual whole foods during the cooking and preparation process.

Trash bowl: Used for containing scraps from cutting, peeling and pitting whole foods, limiting trips walking to the trash can. Place it near the cutting board when preparing whole foods.

Rubber spatula: Used for scraping out purées from the blender/food processor.

Freezer trays (6): Used for freezing baby food purées into cubes. Although any ice cube trays can be used, my favorite freezer trays are those shown here. These trays are made of silicone and each holds 15 cubes, at 1 fl oz (2 T) per cube.

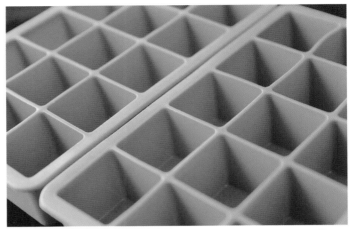

Freezer Trays

These trays are perfect for making baby food for several reasons: (1) silicone is a food-safe material, with no-BPAs or other plastic chemicals to worry about leaching into baby's food; (2) the flexible silicone material allows the frozen purée cubes to dislodge very easily; (3) the trays have a lip around the edge, allowing them to be stackable in the freezer without causing any spills; (4) they are compact, taking up minimal freezer space; (5) they produce perfect cube shapes, which (other than being cute) accommodate very compact, neatly organized storage in freezer bags; (6) recipes in this book have been written to produce quantities to fill 1 of theses trays. A total of 6 of these trays, or their equivalent, will be needed to use *The RealSmart Strategy™*.

Freezer storage bags (1-quart sized): Used for storing frozen baby food purée cubes after dislodging them from freezer trays. Take care to use *freezer storage bags*, as opposed to regular plastic storage bags. Freezer storage bags are made with thicker plastic and perform much better at preventing moisture loss and freezer burn, allowing longer storage time for frozen purée cubes.

Freezer storage basket: Used for organizing and storing all bags of frozen baby food purée cubes (see photo on page 41).

Gloves: Gloves are recommended to protect your hands from cold when transferring frozen baby food purée cubes into freezer storage bags. I recommend wearing a thin insulating glove to protect hands from the cold, then wearing disposable gloves (approved for food handling) on top of the insulating gloves to protect them from getting wet and soiled.

Plastic wrap: Used for covering freezer trays during initial freezing.

Storage containers with lids: Used for a variety of purposes: thawing frozen baby food cubes in the refrigerator; taking baby food on-the-go; organizing meals; serving meals; and storing ground cereal grains. Glass storage bowls work well because you can see what is inside of them, and glass is a perfectly food-

Glass Storage Containers

safe material. In addition, tempered glass storage bowls (manufactured by Pyrex®, Anchor Hocking®) are oven safe, freezer safe and dishwasher safe. Stainless steel storage containers are also a good option. Like glass, stainless steel is a perfectly food-safe material. Stainless steel containers are typically lighter weight than glass containers, making this type more ideal for taking food on-the-go. I recommend having at least 3 storage containers on hand for thawing purée cubes in the refrigerator. In addition, each *dry grind* whole food in your menu (grains, lentils, split peas) will require one 2-cup capacity container for storage.

Baby spoon: For feeding baby.

Water container: Used for baby to start learning how to self-quench thirst. At around the time that solid foods are introduced, baby should also be introduced to drinking water. Consider purchasing a stainless steel container to forgo the worry about BPAs and other plastic chemicals. Stainless steel water containers are more expensive than plastic sippy cups, but in addition to being safer, they last a lot longer. My oldest son has used the same stainless steel container for over 6 years.

Selecting a Menu of Whole Foods

The first step of *The RealSmart Strategy*™ is to choose the whole foods you would like to use to create your 3-month supply of baby food. Refer to *RealSmart Recipes*™ in **Chapter 7** to choose a total of 18 different fruits, vegetables and legumes to purée, plus 2–3 whole grains to grind, taking care to choose foods that encompass a rainbow of colors. I recommend the following quantities of whole food categories to allow optimal flexibility for creating flavorful, nutritionally balanced meals:

Whole Food Category	Quantity
Fruits	8-9
Vegetables	6-7
Legumes*	3-4
	18 (Total)
Whole Grains	2-3

* Lentils and split peas are specific legumes that can be included in addition to the list of 18 whole foods described; these legumes are prepared like whole grains (using the technique of dry grinding) and do not require use of freezer trays for preparation.

You may want to refer to the *Flavor Compatibility Charts* in **Chapter 5** when making whole food selections, as you will gradually begin combining these individual whole foods into balanced meals. Following is a sample menu of whole foods. Additional *RealSmart Strategy*™ examples will be provided based on this specific menu.

RealSmart Whole Foods Menu

Fruits	Vegetables	Legumes	Grains
Apples	Broccoli	Black Beans	Brown Rice
Avocados	Butternut Squash	Haricots Verts	Oats
Bananas	Carrots	Red Lentils	Quinoa
Blueberries	Kale	Sweet Peas	
Cherries	Parsnips		
Mangoes	Sweet Potatoes		
Peaches			
Pears			
Prunes			

Instead of creating your own menu, you may use this
sample *RealSmart Whole Foods Menu* and accompanying
tools *(RealSmart Shopping List* and *RealSmart Mise en
Place Plan)* described in the following sections. As an
added benefit, a sample *3-Month Menu of Meals* based
on this *RealSmart Whole Foods Menu* is also provided
(pages 80-83). Alternatively, you may choose to use
the *RealSmart Whole Foods Menu* as a template, and
substitute any whole food as desired (e.g. substitute
spinach for kale, pumpkin for butternut squash, apricots
for peaches, pinto beans for black beans, etc.).

Preparing a Shopping List

After selecting your menu of whole foods, the next step is to prepare your shopping list. A sample shopping list, based on the *RealSmart Whole Foods Menu,* is provided below. To manually create your own shopping list, refer to *RealSmart Recipes*™ in **Chapter 7** for quantities and other details of whole foods needed. Your list can include an indication of which foods may be found frozen if unavailable fresh, notes on how to select fresh individual produce, whether or not organic is necessary, substitutions you will use if some foods are not available, etc. To help facilitate the creation of your custom shopping list, a free printable shopping list template is available at www.RealSmartBabyFood.com. The *RealSmart Shopping List* shown below is also available to print.

RealSmart Shopping List

WHOLE FOOD	AMOUNT	AVAILABLE FROZEN?**	DIRTY DOZEN™*	CLEAN 15™*	SELECTION TIPS
Apples	1.5 lb (or 4 med)		X		Avoid tart varieties. Choose: Golden/Red Delicious, Gala, Fuji, Jonagold, Braeburn; firm with no bruising
Avocados	1.5 lb (or 3 med)			X	Gently squeeze for slight softness; tight skin, no spotting, no aroma
Bananas	1.5 lb (or 5 med)				Cavendish, yellow, not a lot of brown or green
Blueberries	1 pint (or 16 oz)	X	X		Firm, dry, plump, smooth skins, no mold, white bloom
Cherries	1 lb	X			Taste for sweetness; firm with no wrinkles
Mangoes	1.5 lb (or 2 large)	X		X	Smell at stem end for mango aroma; should yield to gentle pressure
Peaches	1.5 lb	X	X		Soft, not too firm, no green color, peach aroma
Pears	1.5 lb (or 4 med)				Bartletts, or Anjous, Bosc, Comice, Asian; smell and apply pressure just below stem for light softness

WHOLE FOOD	AMOUNT	AVAILABLE FROZEN?**	DIRTY DOZEN™*	CLEAN 15™*	SELECTION TIPS
Prunes	0.3 lb (or 15)				No additives (sulfites, sugar); already pitted
Broccoli	1 lb florets	X			Firm, compact florets; dark green, no brown or yellow
Butternut Squash	1.25 lb	X			Intact stem, dull colored skin, no shiny skin or bruising
Carrots	1.25 lb				Thin, smooth shape, bright color, greens not wilted; not soft or rubbery
Kale	1.5 lb w/ ribs or 1 lb loose leaf	X	X		Deep green, no yellow, brown or wilting; small–med leaves
Parsnips	1.25 lb				Choose smallest, whitest
Sweet Potatoes	1.25 lb			X	Garnet, Jewel, Beauregard; firm, no decay
Black Beans	Two, 15 oz cans				No salt; BPA-free liner (e.g. Eden organic brand)
Haricots Verts	1 lb	X	X		Bright green, crisp, thin, not too stiff
Red Lentils	1 cup				Dry, firm, clean, unwrinkled, uniform color
Sweet Peas	2 lb fresh pods	X		X	Pods: small, firm, green, with no yellow or wilting; Peas: bright green, small, firm. Taste for sweetness.
Brown Rice	1 cup				Check use-by date; smell bulk container
Oats	1 cup				Whole groats, steel cut or rolled; check use-by date; smell bulk container
Quinoa	1 cup				Check use-by date; smell bulk container

*The Environmental Working Group recommends purchasing organic versions of produce on the *Dirty Dozen Plus*™ list, while indicating organic may not be necessary for produce on the *Clean 15*™ list (see page 94).

**If selecting frozen, purchase 16 oz (1 lb)

Go to **www.RealSmartBabyFood.com** to print out this *RealSmart Shopping List* or a blank shopping list template for your customization.

Step 3

Creating Space

After the shopping list has been developed, the next step is to create space for storing the whole foods you plan to bring home. Make sure to have adequate refrigerator, freezer and/or counter storage space available. Refer to the photo on page 41 to visualize the actual quantity of whole foods to be purchased.

Once the whole foods have been puréed, available freezer space is necessary for the initial freezing process of making frozen purée cubes. Sufficient freezer space to store 6 freezer trays after each cooking session is necessary. The stackable silicone freezer trays used in this book (see page 44) each measure 4.5" wide x 7.25" deep x 1.25" tall. Once frozen, purée cubes will need to be transferred from their freezer trays to labeled freezer storage bags, which should then be organized in a freezer storage basket for easy handling (refer to page 57 for photos of this process). The freezer storage basket used in this book to hold a 3-month supply of baby food measures 11.75" wide x 12.5" deep x 7.5" tall (page 41). Measure and clear out space appropriately in your freezer to accommodate frozen purée cubes as described.

Step 4

Shopping

Bring the shopping list created in *Step 2* and head out to do your shopping! Bring your whole foods home and store appropriately until ready for preparation. Refer to **Section 3** for tips on selection, storage and controlling ripening of individual whole foods.

Creating a Mise en Place Plan

After all whole foods have been procured, the next step is to make an organized plan for preparing them. *Mise en place* (pronounced "meez ahn plahs") is a French term that literally means "put into place". This phrase is universally used among personal chefs and food professionals to refer to getting "everything in place" before beginning food preparation. A mise en place plan details what equipment, tools and ingredients are going to be used, what is going to be done, and in what order, allowing you, the chef, to work most efficiently. A mise en place plan will help to avoid last minute realizations that something was forgotten. I recommend preparing the plan after you do your shopping, just in case last minute whole food substitutions have to be made due to lack of availability.

A sample mise en place plan based on the *RealSmart Whole Foods Menu* is provided on the following pages. Go to www.RealSmartBabyFood.com to print out a mise en place template, and use the following tips to develop a mise en place plan tailored to your specific menu.

- Divide individual whole foods equally among the 3 cooking sessions by evenly spreading out *no-cook recipes* (which take the least amount of time), and recipes with longer cook times (e.g. winter squash, root vegetables), in order to keep the timing of each session balanced at approximately 1 hour. Each session should use 6 whole food recipes requiring freezer trays (all recipes except *dry grind recipes* require freezer trays).

- Make sure all necessary equipment and cooking tools are written into the mise en place plan.

- Plan to thaw any frozen no-cook foods by the time the cooking session begins (frozen foods that will be cooked do not need to be thawed before hand).

- Avoid being idle by planning to prepare *no-cook recipes* and doing other tasks while foods are cooking.

- Plan to grind grains, lentils, and/or split peas at the beginning of a cooking session, to ensure availability of a dry blender/food processor bowl.

- Foods that take the longest time to cook should be started first.

RealSmart Mise en Place Plan

Tools Needed	
Blender/Food Processor	Rubber Spatula
Steamer	6 Prep Bowls
Small Pot w/ Lid	Trash Bowl
6 Freezer Trays	4 Storage Containers w/ Lids
Colander	Plastic Wrap
Cutting Board	18 Freezer Storage Bags (1 qt)
Knife	Timer
Vegetable Peeler	Gloves (2 sets: insulating & disposable)
Cherry Pitter (optional)	Freezer Storage Basket

RealSmart Mise en Place Plan

Cooking Session 1

—NO-COOK—	—STEAM—	—HEAT/STEEP—	—DRY GRIND—
Bananas Blueberries	Carrots Apples Haricots verts Sweet Peas		Brown rice

TIME	INACTIVE TASKS	ACTIVE TASKS
Before beginning		• Label freezer storage bags • Shell sweet peas (if using fresh)
Start	Heat water in steamer to a simmer	**Wash:** blueberries, carrots, apples, haricots verts, sweet peas **Peel:** bananas, carrots, apples **Cut:** carrots, apples, haricots verts
10 min	Steam carrots (8–10 min)	**Grind:** rice **Purée and pour:** bananas
20 min	Steam apples (5–7 min)	**Purée and pour:** blueberries, carrots
30 min	Steam haricots verts (5 min) Steam sweet peas (2–3 min)	**Purée and pour:** apples
40 min		**Purée and pour:** haricots verts, sweet peas **Cover and freeze trays**
50 min		• Transfer frozen purée cubes into labeled storage bags
24 hrs later		• Organize filled storage bags in freezer basket & store in freezer
60 min		

A quick rinse of the blender is all that is necessary between purées.

RealSmart Mise en Place Plan
Cooking Session 2

NO-COOK	STEAM	HEAT/STEEP	DRY GRIND
Cherries Mangoes	Sweet potatoes Parsnips Pears	Prunes	Oats

TIME	INACTIVE TASKS	ACTIVE TASKS
Before beginning		• Label freezer storage bags • Pit cherries (if using fresh)
Start	• Heat water in steamer to a simmer • Heat water (2 c) for prunes in small pot to a simmer	**Wash:** cherries, mangoes, sweet potatoes, parsnips, pears **Peel:** mangoes, sweet potatoes, parsnips, pears **Cut:** sweet potatoes
10 min	• Steam sweet potatoes (15 min) • Steep prunes (10 min)	**Cut:** mangoes, parsnips, pears **Grind:** oats
20 min	Steam parsnips (8–10 min)	**Purée and pour:** cherries, mangoes
30 min	Steam pears (5–7 min)	**Purée and pour:** prunes, sweet potatoes
40 min		**Purée and pour:** parsnips, pears **Cover and freeze trays**
50 min		
24 hrs later		• Transfer frozen purée cubes into labeled storage bags • Organize filled storage bags in freezer basket & store in freezer
60 min		

RealSmart Mise en Place Plan
Cooking Session 3

—NO-COOK—	—STEAM—	—HEAT/STEEP—	—DRY GRIND—
Avocados	Butternut squash	Black beans	Quinoa
Peaches	Broccoli		Lentils
	Kale		

TIME	INACTIVE TASKS	ACTIVE TASKS
Before beginning		• Label freezer storage bags
Start		**Wash:** black beans, avocados, kale, butternut squash, peaches, broccoli **Peel:** butternut squash **Cut:** avocados, peaches, broccoli, kale, butternut squash
10 min	• Heat water in steamer to a simmer • Heat water (1 c) for black beans in small pot to a simmer	
	• Steam butternut squash (7-10 min) • Heat black beans (5 min)	**Grind:** quinoa, lentils **Purée and pour:** avocados
20 min	Steam broccoli (6-8 min)	**Purée and pour:** peaches, black beans
30 min	Steam kale (3-5 min x2)	**Purée and pour:** butternut squash
40 min		**Purée and pour:** broccoli, kale **Cover and freeze trays**
50 min		
24 hrs later		• Transfer frozen purée cubes into labeled storage bags
60 min		• Organize filled storage bags in freezer basket & store in freezer

Cooking Sessions

Now that everything is prepared and planned, you are ready to make baby food! Allocate time to perform each of your three 1-hour cooking sessions. Start each cooking session with your specific mise en place plan and individual whole food recipes available for referencing. Read the mise en place plan and recipes from start to finish, then begin implementing the plan, laying out all equipment and ingredients before beginning. Each cooking session will involve preparing 6 whole food purées plus 1 or more whole foods to grind.

When the first cooking session is finished, the purées will need to freeze for at least 24 hours (or until completely solid). The second and third cooking sessions can start any time after the frozen purée cubes have been transferred into freezer storage bags, at which time the freezer trays will be available for use again. By the time session 3 is completely finished, you should have 3-months worth of baby food made, compactly stored, and be ready to start feeding baby!

Wash ··········▶ Peel ··········▶ Cut ··········

Cooking Session Process

Purée and pour ◀··········· Steam ·······

Cover and freeze ····▶ Transfer cubes ·······▶ Store bags and freeze

Chapter 5
Building RealSmart Meals

Once all of the whole food purées have been prepared, you are ready to start planning to build meals. If you have followed *The RealSmart Strategy*™, the quantity of whole food purées and ground whole grain cereals that you have created should be enough to feed baby for approximately 3 months. In order to effectively use your supply of whole food purées to build meals, I recommend meal planning on both a daily and weekly basis.

Daily Meal Planning

Meal planning on a daily basis allows you to be prepared for each day, avoiding last minute decisions on what to feed baby, and being left with frozen purée cubes that need to be quickly thawed. The best way to prepare for meals is to select meals for baby according to your weekly menu (described on the following pages) the night before. Place frozen purée cubes for each meal in a separate container with a lid and store in the refrigerator overnight to thaw. Meals will be thawed and ready to eat the next day. Most purées do not require heating and can be consumed at cool or room temperature (see pages 36-38 for food safety tips). If taking meals on-the-go, just grab your pre-packed containers right out of the refrigerator and take them with you. If you do not take the time to thaw frozen purée cubes the night before, you can still thaw cubes on the stovetop directly in a small pot over low heat. Frozen purée cubes may also be microwaved, though I do not personally recommend this approach, as unnecessary nutrient loss may result.

Meal planning on a weekly basis allows you to see a feeding plan for baby over the course of one week, making it easier for you to ensure that a well balanced, diverse assortment of foods is offered over a set period of time. Weekly meal planning involves creating a written menu plan, indicating foods intended for baby to eat each day of the given week. Weekly menu plans should vary each week, with meal plans becoming progressively more complex as baby grows and his palate develops. In the early stages of introducing solid food purées, baby will begin eating just one food per day, one time per day. Eventually baby will be eating 3 meals per day, with multiple whole foods given at each meal. A sample *3-Month Menu of Meals* is provided later in this chapter (pages 80-83). When creating weekly menu plans, remember the following:

One At a Time, Then Combine

Introduce new foods one at a time in order to screen for allergies. Offer new foods for 3–5 days before introducing another new food. Once the new food is known to be tolerated, it can be combined with other foods. See **Chapter 2** for more details on screening for allergies.

FaT CaN (Flavor and Texture, Color and Nutrients)

Baby's meals should be *flavorful*, with the appropriate *texture*, made of whole foods from every *color* of the rainbow, while keeping *nutrients* in mind. A brief overview of *FaT CaN* is provided below. Refer back to pages 18–24 for more details.

● **Flavor:**

If you are feeding your baby whole foods that you have minimally processed at home according to the recipes in this book, you are already starting off with a flavorful base of individual whole foods. As baby's eating experience progresses, individual whole foods should be combined to form larger, more complex meals. Use the

Flavor Compatibility Charts provided in this chapter as a guide for combining individual whole foods for tasty flavor combinations.

● **Texture:**

Always make sure the texture of baby's meals is appropriate for his specific stage of eating, remembering that no matter how flavorful the food is, if the texture is too lumpy or chunky during the early stages of introducing solid foods, the food will likely be rejected. If you suspect a purée to be too thick, thin it out with water, breast milk or formula. If it is too chunky, it will need to be puréed further. If a purée is too thin, thicken it up with whole grain cereal or pair it with a thicker food.

● **Color:**

Offer whole foods from every color of the rainbow over the course of a week, ensuring that baby receives a wide variety of phytonutrients.

● **Nutrients:**

Be mindful of nutrients being supplied in the meals that you create for baby, paying specific attention to protein, iron, vitamin C (which enhances the absorption of iron), and calcium. Also remember not to restrict dietary intake of fat or calories (specifically when obtained from natural sources) during the first 2 years of life (because *FaT CaN be healthy!*).

In addition to the fruit, vegetable and legume purées, and ground whole grain cereals you have created, baby's meals can be complemented with additional add-ons and mix-ins. Use these complementary foods to increase nutrient density, boost flavor, and/or add texture to baby's meals.

Yogurt

Full-fat plain yogurt should be the choice yogurt for baby. Pre-packaged flavored yogurts are filled with unnecessary sugar. Naturally sweetened, fully flavored yogurts can easily be created by mixing plain yogurt with any fruit purées. Make a simple yogurt meal for baby with the proportion of **1 tablespoon plain yogurt: 1 frozen purée fruit cube**. Thaw purée as usual, then mix with yogurt. Add additional mix-ins described on the following pages if desired. For a special treat, and when baby is a little bit older (12 + months), yogurt can be further sweetened with a dash of maple syrup or agave nectar.

Eggs

Eggs are one of the most nutritionally dense whole foods available and they can be prepared in a variety of ways. The beginning eater can eat hard cooked egg yolks that have been smashed and combined with purées (to prepare, hard boil a whole egg, and use only yolk portion for baby). When baby can handle finger foods (9–11 months), offer sliced or diced whole hard boiled eggs or scrambled eggs. If you are concerned with egg allergies, offer baby only cooked egg yolks, as the common allergy concern is limited to the protein in egg whites.

Ground Nuts & Seeds

Nuts and seeds are supremely nutritious whole foods, providing a wide assortment of nutrients. If you are not concerned with allergies (see page 28), nuts and seeds can safely be given to baby if they are finely ground. A coffee grinder works best to pulse small quantities of nuts and seeds until finely ground, though a blender or food processor can also be used (be careful not to over process or you will create a butter!). Some nuts and seeds can be purchased pre-ground, and will typically be labeled as "meal" (e.g. ground flax seed is usually labeled as "flax meal"). Grind small quantities of whole nuts or seeds at a time (1/2–1 cup), and store in an airtight container for later use. Due to their highly nutritious oil content, nuts and seeds should be stored in the freezer or refrigerator to prevent rancidity, especially after grinding. Start with 1/4 tsp ground nuts or seeds mixed with any purée or yogurt, and progressively increase amount as desired. Always choose nuts and seeds without any added salt for baby.

Some nuts and seeds to choose from include the following:

Nuts	Seeds
Peanuts*	Pumpkin Seed (pepitas)
Almonds	Flax Seed
Cashew Nuts	Sunflower Seed
Walnuts	Sesame Seed
Pistachios	Hemp Seed
Pecans	Chia Seed
Brazil Nuts	
Macadamias	

*technically legumes

Nut & Seed Butters

When baby is ready for finger foods, nut and seed butters can be safely given when spread very thinly on toast or crackers. Butters that are too thick can be a choking hazard, so be sure to spread butters thinly. Nut and seed butters can be made out of any nut or seed by sufficiently grinding and puréeing them into a butter. Many different nut and seed butters can be readily purchased, including peanut butter, almond butter, cashew nut butter, sunflower butter and sesame butter (tahini). Bulk sections of some grocery stores also have a "grind your own" butter station where you can grind fresh nuts or seeds in-store. If purchasing pre-made butters, choose butters that are made from only one ingredient: the nut or seed. Pre-made butters often contain salt and other vegetable oils, which are unnecessary ingredients. Nut and seed butters can be created at home, but it's a tough job for the machine used to do the processing. Be sure to check the owner's manual of your machine before attempting to make nut and seed butters, avoiding the possibility of potentially damaging your machine (a high-speed blender, such as the Vitamix®, can easily and safely create nut and seed butters).

Cheeses

When baby is ready for finger foods, semi-hard cheeses (Cheddar, Colby-Jack, Monterey Jack, etc.) can be given in the form of shreds, or in small cubes. Additional cheeses to offer baby include cottage cheese and ricotta cheese, which can be mixed into fruit, vegetable or legume purées. A variety of cheeses can also be melted into vegetable and legume purées for added texture, flavor and nutrients. Remember to avoid raw-milk cheeses, which are made from unpasteurized milk and may contain very harmful pathogens.

Meat and Fish

While it is possible to purée meats and fish for baby, I prefer not to, as puréeing cooked meat results in a sticky paste that is rather unappetizing to the senses. I prefer to save the introduction of meat and fish for when baby is ready for finger foods, at which time they are ready to eat a similar meat texture as the rest of the family. Whichever method you choose, meat or fish should always be thoroughly cooked (see page 37), and cut/sized appropriately to avoid choking (see page 26). To be efficient, rather than planning to cook meat or fish specifically for baby, offer baby meat that has already been cooked from the family meal. Ground, shredded or finely diced meats (beef, turkey, chicken, lamb, pork, fish) are the most appropriate textures for baby. Do not offer processed deli meats to baby, which are typically high in salt and other preservatives.

Wheat Germ

Wheat germ is the most nutrient dense part of the wheat kernel. When wheat is milled to create white flour, the germ is removed from the wheat kernel (along with the bran), which is why white flours are considered less nutritious than whole wheat. Wheat germ is a particularly excellent source of vitamin E. Sprinkle it on any baby food purée. Wheat germ can be readily found in the baking section or bulk section of most supermarkets. Due to its highly nutritious oil content, wheat germ will readily go rancid, so check the use-by date before purchasing, and store in the refrigerator to extend shelf-life. Start with 1/4 tsp wheat germ mixed with any purée or yogurt, and progressively increase amount as desired.

Nutritional Yeast

Nutritional yeast is an inactive yeast full of B-vitamins and minerals. Nutritional yeast (also called "nooch") is made from the yeast *Saccharomyces cerevisiae*, which is grown on molasses, then harvested, washed, and dried with heat to "inactivate" it. Nutritional yeast is *not* the same as brewer's yeast, baker's yeast or Torula yeast (none of which should be substituted for each other, since they all have different properties). Some nutritional yeast is fortified with vitamin B12 (check the label to confirm), making this a staple in the diet of many vegans. The flavor of nutritional yeast can be described as nutty, cheesy, savory and umami. Nutritional yeast can be found in a flake or powder form in the bulk or dried goods section of any health food store and some supermarkets. Start with 1/4 tsp nutritional yeast mixed with any purée or yogurt, and progressively increase amount as desired.

Dried Seaweed

Dried seaweed contains many minerals. There are several different types of seaweed (sea vegetables), but the most appropriate for babies is *nori*. Nori is a common seaweed used to roll sushi. To prepare ground nori, tear 1–2 sheets of nori into pieces and grind in a coffee grinder or small bowl of a food processor. Nori will have a naturally salty flavor profile. Nori can be found in the Asian section of most supermarkets. Start with 1/4 tsp ground dried seaweed mixed with any purée, and progressively increase amount as desired.

Coconut

Coconuts are an often overlooked source of nutrition and flavor. Coconuts offer a wonderful natural source of fat, fiber and minerals. Fresh, whole coconuts are particularly flavorful, but they can be extremely difficult to open and handle, so I recommend pre-packaged dehydrated (dried), shredded coconut. For baby, choose finely shredded coconut, with no additional ingredients added (such as sulfites). Dehydrated coconut can be found in the bulk or baking section of most supermarkets. Start with 1/4 tsp finely shredded coconut mixed with any purée or yogurt, and progressively increase amount as desired.

Herbs and Spices

Purées can be mildly seasoned with herbs and spices of your choice. Thaw purées as usual, then add a pinch (1/8 tsp or less) of desired dry seasoning. Finely chopped fresh herbs can also be used. Cinnamon, nutmeg, mint, oregano, ginger and curry powder are all tasty examples to start with.

Whole Grains

The beginning eater will need to consume whole grains in the form of cereals, where whole grains are ground into a flour, and the flour is then used to make a cereal (see page 154). Start by offering 1 tablespoon prepared whole grain cereal per meal, mixed with fruit, vegetable or legume purées as desired. Increase amounts of prepared cereal as baby's appetite increases.

When baby is ready for increased textures, whole grains, in their unground form, can be added to purées in lieu of ground cereals. Prepare the whole grain of choice and gently mix with fruit, vegetable or legume purées. In addition to grains mentioned on page 154 to make cereals (rice, oats, quinoa, buckwheat, millet, barley, Kamut®), other whole grains to introduce include couscous, polenta and pasta. A cooking guide for preparing whole grains is provided below.

Cooking Guide for Whole Grains (Unground)

Whole Grain	Grain to Water Ratio	Basic Cooking Method
Brown Rice (long grain)	1 cup : 2 cups	Simmer 45 min.
Oats (rolled)	1 cup : 2 cups	Start grain in cold water, then simmer 15 min.
Oats (steel cut)	1 cup : 4 cups	Start grain in cold water, then simmer 30 min.
Oats (whole groats)	1 cup : 3 cups	Start grain in cold water, then simmer 1-1.5 hrs.
Buckwheat (Kasha)	1 cup : 2 cups	Simmer 20 min.
Barley	1 cup : 3.5 cups	Simmer 1 hr.
Millet	1 cup : 2.5 cups	Simmer 30 min, remove from heat, fluff and let sit uncovered for 20 min.
Kamut®	1 cup : 3 cups	Soak overnight in cold water. Drain, then simmer with fresh water 45 min.
Quinoa	1 cup : 2 cups	Rinse before cooking. Simmer 20 min.
Couscous (whole wheat)	1 cup : 1.5 cups	Bring water to boil, add couscous, cover and remove from heat. Let sit until water absorbs (5-10 min). Fluff with fork.
Polenta	1 cup : 4 cups	Bring water to boil, add polenta in slow stream. Constantly stir to prevent clumps and simmer 30 min.

Flavor Compatibility Charts

Use the following *Flavor Compatibility Charts* as a guide for combining whole foods for optimal flavor when building meals. These charts were designed for each whole food featured in *RealSmart Recipes*™ (**Chapter 7**). Each column highlights an individual whole food, and lists complementary whole foods that combine well with it to produce a flavorful meal. These lists are a general guide and by no means comprehensive, so feel free to be adventurous and create your own combinations.

Multiple whole foods within any given column can be combined. Start by combining frozen purée cubes within any column in a 1:1 ratio. For example, by looking at the *Apples* column, you will see that 1 cube apples can be combined with 1 cube carrots. For a more complex meal, 1 cube apples can be combined with 1 cube carrots and 1 cube kale.

If you find that baby does not like any given meal combination due to particularly strong flavors, adding an additional cube of fruit for enhanced sweetness often does the trick. Do not forget to add whole grain cereals when building meals, which are not included here. The neutral flavor of most whole grains pairs well with just about anything. Additional flavor complements include any of the *RealSmart Add-ons and Mix-ins* discussed earlier in this chapter.

Apples		Apricots	Asparagus
Apricots	Lentils	Apples	Bananas
Avocados	Mangoes	Bananas	Carrots
Bananas	Nectarines	Blackberries	Parsnips
Beets	Papaya	Blueberries	Spinach
Black Beans	Parsnips	Carrots	Summer Squash
Blackberries	Peaches	Cherries	Sweet Peas
Blueberries	Pears	Mangoes	
Broccoli	Pinto Beans	Nectarines	
Cannellini Beans	Plums/Prunes	Papaya	
Cantaloupe	Raspberries	Peaches	
Carrots	Spinach	Pears	
Chard	Split Peas	Plums/Prunes	
Cherries	Strawberries	Raspberries	
Figs	Summer Squash	Strawberries	
Garbanzo Beans	Sweet Peas		
Green Beans	Sweet Potatoes		
Honeydew Melon	Turnips		
Kale	Winter Squash		
Kiwifruit			

Avocados	Bananas		Beets
Apples	Apples	Mangoes	Apples
Bananas	Apricots	Nectarines	Carrots
Black Beans	Asparagus	Papaya	Edamame
Blackberries	Avocados	Parsnips	Garbanzo Beans
Blueberries	Blackberries	Peaches	Parsnips
Cantaloupe	Blueberries	Pears	Pears
Honeydew Melon	Broccoli	Plums/Prunes	Sweet Potatoes
Mangoes	Cantaloupe	Raspberries	Winter Squash
Nectarines	Carrots	Spinach	
Papaya	Chard	Split Peas	
Peaches	Cherries	Strawberries	
Pears	Figs	Summer Squash	
Pinto Beans	Green Beans	Sweet Peas	
Raspberries	Honeydew Melon	Sweet Potatoes	
Strawberries	Kale	Watermelon	
	Kiwifruit	Winter Squash	

Black Beans	Blackberries	Blueberries	Broccoli
Apples	Apples	Apples	Apples
Avocado	Apricots	Apricots	Bananas
Carrots	Avocados	Avocados	Cannellini Beans
Mangoes	Bananas	Bananas	Carrots
Papaya	Blueberries	Blackberries	Garbanzo Beans
Parsnips	Cantaloupe	Cantaloupe	Lentils
Pears	Carrots	Carrots	Parsnips
Summer Squash	Figs	Cherries	Pears
Sweet Potatoes	Honeydew Melon	Figs	Plums/Prunes
Winter Squash	Kiwifruit	Honeydew Melon	Sweet Potatoes
	Mangoes	Kiwifruit	Winter Squash
	Nectarines	Mangoes	
	Papaya	Nectarines	
	Peaches	Papaya	
	Pears	Peaches	
	Plums/Prunes	Pears	
	Raspberries	Plums/Prunes	
	Strawberries	Raspberries	
	Watermelon	Strawberries	
		Watermelon	

Cannellini Beans	Cantaloupe	Carrots	Chard
Apples	Apples	Apples	Apples
Broccoli	Avocados	Apricots	Bananas
Carrots	Bananas	Asparagus	Cannellini Beans
Chard	Blackberries	Bananas	Carrots
Kale	Blueberries	Beets	Garbanzo Beans
Parsnips	Honeydew Melon	Black Beans	Lentils
Pears	Kiwifruit	Blackberries	Parsnips
Spinach	Mangoes	Blueberries	Peaches
Summer Squash	Papaya	Broccoli	Pears
Sweet Potatoes	Pears	Cannellini Beans	Strawberries
Winter Squash	Raspberries	Chard	Sweet Potatoes
	Strawberries	Edamame	Winter Squash
	Watermelon	Garbanzo Beans	
		Green Beans	
		Kale	
		Lentils	
		Parsnips	
		Pears	
		Pinto Beans	
		Plums/Prunes	
		Raspberries	
		Spinach	
		Split Peas	
		Summer Squash	
		Sweet Peas	
		Turnips	

Cherries	Edamame	Figs	Garbanzo Beans
Apples	Beets	Apples	Apples
Apricots	Carrots	Bananas	Beets
Bananas	Parsnips	Blackberries	Broccoli
Blueberries	Summer Squash	Blueberries	Carrots
Kiwifruit	Sweet Potatoes	Pears	Chard
Mangoes	Winter Squash	Raspberries	Kale
Nectarines		Strawberries	Parsnips
Papaya			Pears
Peaches			Spinach
Pears			Summer Squash
Plums/Prunes			Sweet Potatoes
Summer Squash			Winter Squash
Winter Squash			

Green Beans	Honeydew Melon	Kale	Kiwifruit
Apples	Apples	Apples	Apples
Bananas	Avocados	Bananas	Bananas
Carrots	Bananas	Cannellini Beans	Blackberries
Nectarines	Blackberries	Carrots	Blueberries
Parsnips	Blueberries	Garbanzo Beans	Cantaloupe
Peaches	Cantaloupe	Lentils	Cherries
Pears	Kiwifruit	Parsnips	Honeydew Melon
Summer Squash	Mangoes	Peaches	Mangoes
Sweet Potatoes	Papaya	Pears	Papaya
Winter Squash	Pears	Plums/Prunes	Pears
	Raspberries	Strawberries	Plums/Prunes
	Strawberries	Sweet Potatoes	Raspberries
	Watermelon	Winter Squash	Strawberries
			Watermelon

Lentils	Mangoes	Nectarines	Papaya
Apples	Apples	Apples	Apples
Broccoli	Apricots	Apricots	Apricots
Carrots	Avocados	Avocados	Avocados
Chard	Bananas	Bananas	Bananas
Kale	Black Beans	Blackberries	Black Beans
Parsnips	Blackberries	Blueberries	Blackberries
Pears	Blueberries	Cherries	Blueberries
Spinach	Cantaloupe	Green Beans	Cantaloupe
Summer Squash	Cherries	Mangoes	Cherries
Sweet Potatoes	Honeydew Melon	Papaya	Honeydew Melon
Winter Squash	Kiwifruit	Peaches	Kiwifruit
	Nectarines	Pears	Mangoes
	Papaya	Plums/Prunes	Nectarines
	Peaches	Raspberries	Peaches
	Pears	Strawberries	Pears
	Pinto Beans	Summer Squash	Pinto Beans
	Plums/Prunes	Watermelon	Plums/Prunes
	Raspberries		Raspberries
	Strawberries		Strawberries
	Watermelon		Watermelon

Parsnips	Peaches	Pears	
Apples	Apples	Apples	Kiwifruit
Asparagus	Apricots	Apricots	Lentils
Bananas	Avocados	Avocados	Mangoes
Beets	Bananas	Bananas	Nectarines
Black Beans	Blackberries	Beets	Papaya
Broccoli	Blueberries	Black Beans	Parsnips
Cannellini Beans	Chard	Blackberries	Peaches
Carrots	Cherries	Blueberries	Pinto Beans
Chard	Green Beans	Broccoli	Plums/Prunes
Edamame	Kale	Cannellini Beans	Raspberries
Garbanzo Beans	Mangoes	Cantaloupe	Spinach
Green Beans	Nectarines	Carrots	Split Peas
Kale	Papaya	Chard	Strawberries
Lentils	Pears	Cherries	Summer Squash
Pears	Plums/Prunes	Figs	Sweet Peas
Pinto Beans	Raspberries	Garbanzo Beans	Sweet Potatoes
Plums/Prunes	Spinach	Green Beans	Turnips
Spinach	Strawberries	Honeydew Melon	Winter Squash
Split Peas	Summer Squash	Kale	
Summer Squash	Watermelon		
Sweet Peas			
Sweet Potatoes			
Turnips			
Winter Squash			

Pinto Beans	Plums/ Prunes	Raspberries	Spinach
Apples	Apples	Apples	Apples
Avocados	Apricots	Apricots	Asparagus
Carrots	Bananas	Avocados	Bananas
Mangoes	Blackberries	Bananas	Cannellini Beans
Papaya	Blueberries	Blackberries	Carrots
Parsnips	Broccoli	Blueberries	Garbanzo Beans
Pears	Carrots	Cantaloupe	Lentils
Summer Squash	Cherries	Carrots	Parsnips
Sweet Potatoes	Kale	Figs	Peaches
Winter Squash	Kiwifruit	Honeydew Melon	Pears
	Mangoes	Kiwifruit	Strawberries
	Nectarines	Mangoes	Sweet Potatoes
	Papaya	Nectarines	Winter Squash
	Parsnips	Papaya	
	Peaches	Peaches	
	Pears	Pears	
	Raspberries	Plums/Prunes	
	Strawberries	Strawberries	
		Watermelon	

Split Peas	Strawberries	Summer Squash	Sweet Peas
Apples	Apples	Apples	Apples
Bananas	Apricots	Asparagus	Asparagus
Carrots	Avocados	Bananas	Bananas
Parsnips	Bananas	Black Beans	Carrots
Pears	Blackberries	Cannellini Beans	Parsnips
Summer Squash	Blueberries	Carrots	Pears
Sweet Potatoes	Cantaloupe	Cherries	Summer Squash
Turnips	Chard	Edamame	Sweet Potatoes
Winter Squash	Figs	Garbanzo Beans	Turnips
	Honeydew Melon	Green Beans	Winter Squash
	Kale	Lentils	
	Kiwifruit	Nectarines	
	Mangoes	Parsnips	
	Nectarines	Peaches	
	Papaya	Pears	
	Peaches	Pinto Beans	
	Pears	Split Peas	
	Plums/Prunes	Sweet Peas	
	Raspberries	Sweet Potatoes	
	Spinach	Winter Squash	
	Watermelon		

Sweet Potatoes	Turnips	Watermelon	Winter Squash
Apples	Apples	Bananas	Apples
Bananas	Carrots	Blackberries	Bananas
Beets	Parsnips	Blueberries	Beets
Black Beans	Pears	Cantaloupe	Black Beans
Broccoli	Split Peas	Honeydew Melon	Broccoli
Cannellini Beans	Sweet Peas	Mangoes	Cannellini Beans
Chard	Sweet Potatoes	Nectarines	Chard
Edamame	Winter Squash	Papaya	Cherries
Garbanzo Beans		Peaches	Edamame
Green Beans		Raspberries	Garbanzo Beans
Kale		Strawberries	Green Beans
Lentils			Kale
Parsnips			Lentils
Pears			Parsnips
Pinto Beans			Pears
Spinach			Pinto Beans
Split Peas			Spinach
Summer Squash			Split Peas
Sweet Peas			Summer Squash
Turnips			Sweet Peas
			Turnips

RealSmart 3-Month Menu of Meals

Your individual supply of whole food purées offers the complete freedom to build your own weekly menus as desired. The following pages display a 3-month menu of meals that I created based on the *RealSmart Whole Foods Menu*, referring to the *Flavor Compatibility Charts* to combine individual purées into meals. As you can see, the *RealSmart Strategy*™ can, indeed, create enough baby food to feed baby for a period of 3 months. This 3-month menu displays 175 increasingly complex meals, built from 270 frozen fruit, vegetable and legume purée cubes, plus whole grains, which were prepared from a rainbow of 24 different whole foods (all made in 3 one-hour blocks of time). I told you this plan was smart!

Rainbow of Foods Includes:

- Cherries, Red Lentils
- Sweet Potatoes, Butternut Squash, Mangoes, Carrots
- Peaches, Bananas, Apples, Pears
- Broccoli, Kale, Sweet Peas, Haricots Verts, Avocados
- Blueberries
- Prunes
- Rice, Oats, Quinoa, Flax Seed
- Black Beans
- Parsnips, Yogurt

RealSmart 3-Month Menu of Meals

MONTH 1

		Sunday	Monday	Tuesday	Wednesday	Thursday	Friday	Saturday
WEEK 1	MEAL 1	*sweet potatoes*	*sweet potatoes*	*sweet potatoes*	*sweet potatoes*	*sweet peas*	*sweet peas*	*sweet peas*
WEEK 2	MEAL 1	*bananas*	*bananas*	*bananas*	*butternut squash*	*butternut squash*	*butternut squash*	*butternut squash*
WEEK 3	MEAL 1	*apples*	*apples*	*apples*	*rice cereal* + bananas	*rice cereal* + sweet peas	*rice cereal* + butternut squash	*rice cereal* + apples
WEEK 4	MEAL 1	*avocados*	*avocados*	*avocados*	*parsnips*	*parsnips*	*parsnips*	*parsnips* + rice cereal
	MEAL 2	sweet potatoes + apples	sweet peas + rice cereal	butternut squash + rice cereal	bananas + rice cereal	avocados	sweet peas + rice cereal	butternut squash + apples

MONTH 2

		Sunday	Monday	Tuesday	Wednesday	Thursday	Friday	Saturday
WEEK 5	MEAL 1	*pears*	*pears*	*pears*	*mangoes*	*mangoes*	*mangoes*	*mangoes*
	MEAL 2	avocados	butternut squash + bananas	parsnips + apples	avocados	sweet peas + rice cereal	sweet potatoes + pears	parsnips + rice cereal
WEEK 6	MEAL 1	*broccoli*	*broccoli* + rice cereal	*broccoli* + rice cereal	*broccoli* + rice cereal	*cherries*	*cherries*	*cherries* + rice cereal
	MEAL 2	butternut squash + rice cereal	parsnips + bananas	mangoes + avocados	sweet potatoes + bananas	sweet peas + rice cereal	broccoli + apples	parsnips + pears
WEEK 7	MEAL 1	*oat cereal* + bananas	*oat cereal* + pears	*oat cereal* + cherries	*kale* + bananas	*kale* + apples	*kale* + sweet potatoes	*kale* + pears
	MEAL 2	sweet potatoes + pears	mangoes + cherries	parsnips + apples	broccoli + pears	avocados + mangoes	butternut squash + cherries	mangoes + oat cereal
WEEK 8	MEAL 1	*black beans* + rice cereal	*black beans* + rice cereal	*black beans* + rice cereal	*prunes* + oat cereal	*prunes* + oat cereal	*prunes* + rice cereal	*prunes* + rice cereal
	MEAL 2	avocados + mangoes	sweet peas + sweet potatoes	broccoli + pears	butternut squash + cherries	kale + bananas	sweet potatoes + black beans	parsnips + bananas

RealSmart 3-Month Menu of Meals, based on the *RealSmart Whole Foods Menu* (see page 47). *Italicized* foods indicate foods being introduced as a new food, following the strategy of "*One at a Time, Then Combine.*" Each instance of a whole food appearing on the menu indicates one frozen purée cube of that individual whole food. (Note: yogurt and flax seed are add-ons/mix-ins in addition to the original *RealSmart Whole Foods Menu*).

		Sunday	Monday	Tuesday	Wednesday	Thursday	Friday	Saturday
WEEK 9	MEAL 1	yogurt + bananas	yogurt + mangoes	yogurt + pears	yogurt + prunes	carrots + rice cereal	carrots + kale	carrots + black beans
	MEAL 2	broccoli + pears	sweet peas + parsnips	kale + prunes	bananas + cherries	broccoli + prunes	cherries + yogurt	prunes + yogurt
	MEAL 3	butternut squash + kale	avocados + black beans	sweet peas + butternut squash	parsnips + pears	kale + sweet potatoes	broccoli + parsnips	sweet potatoes + sweet peas
WEEK 10	MEAL 1	peaches + oat cereal	peaches + oat cereal	peaches + oat cereal	haricots verts + rice cereal	haricots verts + rice cereal	haricots verts + rice cereal	haricots verts + carrots
	MEAL 2	cherries + yogurt	prunes + yogurt	carrots + black beans + apples	cherries + oat cereal + yogurt	carrots + sweet peas	prunes + oat cereal + yogurt	black beans + rice cereal + apples
	MEAL 3	sweet peas + carrots + rice cereal	kale + carrots + black beans	broccoli + prunes + rice cereal	carrots + broccoli + rice cereal	avocados + mangoes + black beans	kale + butternut squash + rice cereal	peaches + cherries + oat cereal
WEEK 11	MEAL 1	blueberries + oat cereal	blueberries + oat cereal	blueberries + peaches	red lentils + rice cereal	red lentils + broccoli	red lentils + butternut squash	red lentils + sweet potatoes
	MEAL 2	haricots verts + peaches + rice cereal	parsnips + prunes + rice cereal	haricots verts + carrots + bananas	peaches + blueberries + yogurt	blueberries + peaches + yogurt	sweet peas + carrots + rice cereal	parsnips + haricots verts + rice cereal
	MEAL 3	kale + sweet potatoes + black beans	haricots verts + peaches + rice cereal	avocados + mangoes + black beans	broccoli + haricots verts + pears	haricots verts + apples + rice cereal	kale + apples + haricots verts	avocados + mangoes + black beans
WEEK 12	MEAL 1	quinoa cereal + cherries + blueberries	quinoa cereal + peaches + cherries	quinoa cereal + prunes	flax seed + blueberries + oat cereal	flax seed + blueberries + yogurt	flax seed + blueberries + oat cereal	flax seed + prunes + oat cereal
	MEAL 2	blueberries + peaches + yogurt	pears + blueberries + yogurt	blueberries + yogurt + oat cereal	cherries + peaches + oat cereal	peaches + blueberries + oat cereal	peaches + blueberries + oat cereal	peaches + blueberries + yogurt
	MEAL 3	avocados + mangoes + black beans	kale + carrots + apples + haricots verts	broccoli + prunes + rice cereal	haricots verts + carrots + quinoa cereal	kale + carrots + red lentils + haricots verts	haricots verts + carrots + quinoa cereal	avocados + mangoes + black beans

✳ Remember:

Every baby is different, so there is no one correct amount or strict advice to give regarding quantity of solid foods. Most babies start off eating 1 cube at a time, but some may start off eating 3 cubes at a time! Follow baby's cues. You choose what to feed baby, but let baby decide how much to eat.

RealSmart Meal Favorites

The following pages display 30 meal creations that have been big favorites among many little tasters. Use each meal combination as-is, or as inspiration to create your own. Developing fun meal names makes the eating experience even better! Unless otherwise indicated, whole food ingredients are listed in quantities of 1 frozen purée cube. Increase recipe quantities as desired by increasing amounts of each ingredient proportionally. Use whole grains in full whole grain or ground cereal form, depending on baby's current texture stage. For ground cereal form, start with 1 tablespoon prepared cereal grain (page 155); for full whole grain form, start with 1/4 c cooked whole grain (page 67).

Bean-Ango-Cado:
Black Beans + Mangoes
+ Avocados

Berry Figgy Buckwheat:
Raspberries + Figs
+ Buckwheat

Squashed Cherry Millet:
Butternut Squash
+ Cherries + Millet

Berry Tropical Melon:
Strawberries + Kiwifruit
+ Watermelon

Sweet Parsnips & Peas:
Parsnips + Split Peas
+ Apples

Blue Bango:

Blueberries + Bananas
+ Mangoes

Purple Papaya Flax Yogurt:

Prunes + Papaya + 2 T Yogurt
+ 1/4 tsp Flax Seed (ground)

Berry Kiwi Cooler:

Blackberries + Kiwifruit
+ Cantaloupe

Melon Medley:

Watermelon + Cantaloupe
+ Honeydew Melon

Spring Green Kamut®:

Asparagus + Sweet Peas + Kamut®

Sea-da-mame Rice:

Edamame + Brown Rice
+ 1/4 tsp Seaweed (ground)

Coconutty Mango Lassi:

Mangoes + 1/4 tsp Coconut (finely
shredded) + 1 T Yogurt

Plum Gingered Broccoli Quinoa:

Broccoli + Plums + Quinoa
+ 1/8 tsp Ginger powder

Raspber-Cot Quinoa:

Raspberries + Apricots + Quinoa

Curried Squashed Peas:

Sweet Peas + Butternut Squash
+ 1/8 tsp Curry Powder

Nectar-Squashed Green Beans:

Green Beans + Nectarines
+ Zucchini

Creamy Spiced Spinach:

Spinach + Cannellini Beans
+ 1/8 tsp Nutmeg

Lentil Barley Stew:

Red Lentils + Sweet Potatoes
+ Barley

Rainbow Rice:

Beets + Avocados + Pears
+ Brown Rice

Nutty Apple Oatmeal:

Apples + Oats + 1/4 tsp Almonds
(ground) + 1/8 tsp Cinnamon

Autumn Quinoa:

Sweet Potatoes +
Black Beans + Quinoa

Sweet 'Snipped Chard:

Swiss Chard +
Parsnips + Pears

Turned-up Carrots & Peas:

Carrots + Sweet Peas + Turnips

Minty Peas & Rice:

Sweet Peas + Brown Rice + 1/8 tsp Mint
(fresh, finely chopped)

Red Banana Buckwheat:

Bananas + Cherries + Buckwheat

Green Banana Barley:

Bananas + Spinach + Barley

Pumpkin Pecan Pie:

Pumpkin + Apples
+ 1/4 tsp Pecans (ground)
+ 1/8 tsp Cinnamon

Cheesy Pinto Polenta:

Pinto Beans + Polenta + 1 T Cheddar
(shredded, melted)

Sweet Creamy Kale:

Kale + Sweet Potatoes
+ Garbanzo Beans

Peachy Strawberry Salad:

Peaches
+ Strawberries
+ Spinach

At around 9–11 months of age, baby develops a pincer grasp (the ability to pick up objects with the thumb and forefinger), and finger foods can then be introduced to complement purées. Since baby has a very small airway, finger foods should be cut appropriately to avoid the hazard of choking (see page 26). Some options for finger foods are listed below:

Finger Foods

- Pieces of soft fruits
- Pieces of cooked veggies
- Shredded semi-hard cheeses (Cheddar, Monterey Jack, etc.)
- Whole grain toast
- Shredded or diced meats
- Cooked eggs (scrambled, hard boiled)
- Soft cooked beans
- Whole grain crackers

After the pincer grasp develops, baby will soon be ready to try holding a spoon or fork (though don't expect half of what she tries to get into her mouth to make it in!). It is important to let baby try to feed herself when ready to do so, but it is helpful to offer baby one spoon to work with while you use another to help feed her. Otherwise, until baby increases her coordination, the meal will end up a huge mess with little food actually being consumed.

Eventually baby will be ready to handle the textures of everyday foods and purées will no longer be needed. By that time, baby will have already been introduced to a wide variety of whole foods and flavors, and he will have learned to not only accept, but to enjoy these foods. When the time comes to move beyond purées, continue feeding baby these same foods, just eliminate the step of puréeing. Offer steamed veggies, fruits, whole grains, beans, nuts, seeds, in addition to dairy, eggs, meats and fish. Baby will continue eating these foods as long as they are sufficiently offered.

If baby has moved beyond purées and you find that you have a supply of unused frozen purée cubes left in the freezer, don't throw them out! These frozen purées can be used for a variety purposes. Use fruit purées to flavor plain yogurt, create smoothies, top a cake or moisten baked goods. Add vegetable purées to soups and sauces, or add to the batter of baked goods for a nutrient spike (e.g. zucchini, carrots). Use legume purées to create bean dips (e.g. hummus) or spread directly on toast or a wrap. The list is endless. These are whole foods that have just been puréed. Don't let them go to waste. Enjoy them! In fact, I keep a constant stock of frozen fruit, vegetable and legume purée cubes in my freezer to use for all of the purposes described above.

Fresh figs with fig purée. See recipe, page 120

Section 3

Selecting and Preparing Whole Foods For Baby

Chapter 6
Selection and Preparation Tips

Fresh, Frozen and Canned Foods

When shopping for whole fruits, vegetables and legumes for preparing baby food, fresh is best. When fresh produce is not available, a suitable alternative is frozen fruits, vegetables and legumes. Often times frozen produce can actually have higher nutrient contents than their fresh counterparts because they are harvested at peak ripeness, when nutrients are at their peak, and then immediately frozen, allowing nutrients to remain stable. Fresh produce is often harvested before peak ripeness, and therefore before nutrients have a chance to optimally develop, in order to allow for travel time and shelf time at their final destinations.

Organic frozen produce is a particularly good alternative in locations where specific fresh organic produce is not available. Organic frozen produce can be found in the freezer section of many supermarkets, either next to conventionally grown frozen produce, or in a completely separate location allocated to organic frozen products.

When using frozen produce, it is best to thaw foods completely before puréeing if they will be puréed raw (without cooking). Frozen produce that will be cooked prior to puréeing does not need to be thawed beforehand. All frozen produce should be washed before preparing, just like fresh produce (see **Chapter 3**). Recipes for whole foods that are readily available for purchase as frozen are labeled as *available frozen*. Note that the quantities of many frozen fruits and vegetables needed will differ from the quantities of fresh produce indicated in the recipes of this book, because the skins/rinds and seeds of most frozen produce have already been removed.

Canned fruits and vegetables are not suitable for preparing homemade baby food, as many contain salt or other additives to aid in preservation. Canned products (like jarred baby food) are also subject to very high temperature and pressure treatments, resulting in substantial nutrient, flavor and texture loss.

 Tip

When using frozen fruits, vegetables or legumes, one 16 oz bag will yield approximately one freezer tray, or 15 frozen purée cubes, at 1 fl oz each.

The one exception for using canned foods for preparing baby food is canned beans (pinto beans, black beans, garbanzo beans, etc.). Canned beans are dried beans that have been previously cooked. They are nutritionally equivalent to dried beans that are cooked at home, and they take significantly less time to prepare. Many canned beans are packed with salt, however, so it is necessary to thoroughly rinse and drain beans before using. Preferably, use no- or low-sodium versions of beans when available. Another concern with canned beans (or any other canned product) is that they are typically packed in cans with BPA-liners (liners containing bisphenol A, a controversial chemical found in some plastics and food packaging materials). Read the labels of canned products and look for a statement reading "BPA-Free Lining". Alternatives to BPA liners are more expensive for food companies to use, and if they are using them they will be sure to let you know.*

Use Your Senses

When selecting fruits and vegetables, incorporate all of your senses. Look, feel, smell, taste (many stores will allow you to sample fresh produce if you just ask), and even listen (see tips on selecting melons) before selecting. Avoid produce that has been damaged, bruised, has

*As of the publication of this book, Eden® Organic is the only company that reliably does not use BPA-liners for canned beans.

visible mold, or has an off-odor, such as a fermented smell. One bad avocado can ruin the whole batch of purée.

When to Choose Organic

Whenever possible, purchase organic foods, especially for baby. Consuming foods that have been organically grown will significantly lower exposure to pesticides and chemical contaminants. Babies have tiny little bodies, and still-developing immune systems, leaving them much more susceptible than adults to potential harm from the toxic chemicals and pesticide residues found on most non-organic foods.

When purchasing everything organic is not an option, there is an excellent resource available to help limit your exposure to toxins. The Environmental Working Group (EWG) ranks fruits and vegetables based on their total load of pesticide residues. EWG annually produces two lists to help you determine which fruits and vegetables are most important to buy organic: (1) *Dirty Dozen Plus*™, which lists the 12 most contaminated fruits and vegetables (the Plus category highlights crops that do not meet the traditional *Dirty Dozen*™ criteria but are highly contaminated with highly toxic insecticides), and (2) *Clean 15*™, which lists the 15 least contaminated fruits and vegetables. EWG recommends purchasing organic versions of produce featured on the *Dirty Dozen Plus*™ list, and indicates it may not be necessary to purchase organic versions of produce featured on the *Clean 15*™ list. The 2012 *Dirty Dozen Plus*™ and *Clean 15*™ lists are below. A complete list containing full up-to-date rankings of additional produce can be obtained at www.ewg.org (the full 2012 list analyzed 45 different fruits and vegetables).

Dirty Dozen Plus™
(highest in pesticide residue)

1. Apples
2. Celery
3. Sweet Bell Peppers
4. Peaches
5. Strawberries
6. Nectarines (imported)
7. Grapes (imported)
8. Spinach
9. Lettuce
10. Cucumbers
11. Blueberries (domestic)
12. Potatoes

Plus

+ Green Beans
+ Kale/Leafy Greens

Clean 15™
(lowest in pesticide residue)

1. Onions
2. Sweet Corn
3. Pineapples
4. Avocado
5. Cabbage
6. Sweet peas
7. Asparagus
8. Mangoes
9. Eggplant
10. Kiwifruit
11. Cantaloupe (domestic)
12. Sweet Potatoes
13. Grapefruit
14. Watermelon
15. Mushrooms

Recipes made from whole foods included on the *Dirty Dozen Plus*™ or *Clean 15*™ lists are indicated as *Dirty Dozen Plus*™* and *Clean 15*™ *, respectively.

When choosing meats and animal-derived foods (eggs, dairy), remember that the quality of the product is only as good as the quality of the animal who was used to make it. Standards for organically raised animals include: organic feed, no use of antibiotics or other drugs, sanitary housing conditions, freedom of movement, access to the outdoors, and conditions that accommodate the natural behavior of the animal.

Choose organic dairy products whenever possible to avoid exposure to synthetic hormones and pesticide residues that make their way into non-organic milk. When choosing organic is not possible, consider choosing dairy products that are free of artificial growth hormones. rBGH (recombinant bovine growth hormone), also known as rBST (recombinant bovine somatotropin), is an artificial growth hormone injected into dairy cows to boost milk production (while increasing the incidences of mastitis, lameness, and reproductive complications of the cow). Although regarded as safe by the FDA, the long-term health implications due to consumption of this artificial hormone are still not well understood. All organic dairy products are free of artificial hormones, but many non-organic dairy products are not. To determine if a specific dairy product is free of these hormones, look for a statement on the label indicating the product was produced from cows not treated with rBGH.

Where to Source Whole Foods

Many whole foods can be found at traditional supermarkets. The rule of thumb for shopping for whole foods in the supermarket is to shop the perimeter of the store (processed foods are generally within the middle aisles). Availability of organic foods and less mainstream whole foods, however, is typically limited at traditional supermarkets. If you are fortunate enough to live near a health food market (such as Whole Foods Market®), you will likely find everything you need.

Farmer's markets are an excellent place to find fresh, organic produce. One of the many benefits of shopping at a Farmer's Market is that you have the opportunity to talk directly with the farmer who grew your food. Many small farmers may not be certified organic, but their sustainable farming practices may produce what many refer to as *beyond organic* foods. When you talk to your farmers, you know your farmer, and you know your food. Many local farms also offer CSA (Community Supported Agriculture) programs, where you can choose to be a member. CSA members pay at the beginning of a growing season for a share of the anticipated harvest. Once harvesting begins, members typically receive weekly shares of seasonal vegetables, fruits, herbs, eggs, honey, dairy products and/or meats, depending upon the farm. Of course, you can also start your own garden, large or small, or participate in a community garden.

Controlling Ripening

When selecting fresh fruits and vegetables for preparing homemade baby food, it is important to gauge ripeness according to when you will actually begin preparing the baby food. Fruits and vegetables should be fully ripened at the time of preparation. If you are purchasing whole foods to prepare within 1–2 days, select fully ripened fruits and vegetables. If you will not be preparing baby food for several days, select produce that is not fully ripe, or follow the techniques described in this section to slow down ripening. Some produce can also have the ripening process accelerated, if necessary.

Ethylene is a natural ripening gas produced by many fruits. Some fruits produce ethylene as they ripen *(ethylene producers)*, and other fruits and vegetables are sensitive to it *(ethylene-sensitive)*. Ethylene-sensitive fruits will ripen much faster when placed next to any ethylene producing fruit. Bananas are big ethylene producers. If you want to accelerate ripening of an ethylene-sensitive fruit, place it next to or in a closed paper bag with a banana. If you do not want your ethylene-sensitive fruit to experience accelerated ripening, keep it away from ethylene producers. It is best to always keep ethylene-sensitive *vegetables* away from ethylene producers, because these veggies will discolor and develop undesirable flavor compounds when placed near ethylene producers. Ethylene gas can build up in the refrigerator, which is why storing ethylene-sensitive produce in plastic bags is often recommended. Ethylene producers and ethylene-sensitive produce are listed below and labeled in individual whole food recipes as *Ethylene producer* and *Ethylene-sensitive*, respectively.

Ethylene producers:

Apples, apricots, avocados, bananas, cantaloupe, honeydew melon, kiwifruit, mangoes, nectarines, papayas, peaches, pears, plums, tomatoes.

Ethylene-sensitive:

All ethylene producers (see above), plus: artichoke, asparagus, broccoli, Brussels sprouts, cabbage, carrots, cauliflower, celery, corn, cucumber, green beans, leafy greens (spinach, kale, chard), lettuce, parsley, potatoes, squash, sweet potatoes, melons.

Ripening can also be controlled with temperature. Generally, refrigeration will slow down the ripening process for many fruits and vegetables, and ripening will occur faster when they are left at room temperature.

Natural Variability

It is important to understand that whole fruits and vegetables are
natural products, and there is a natural variability inherent to them.
This variability can be influenced by growing conditions (weather,
soil composition, fertilizer use, sunlight exposure), plant genetics and
storage conditions. Variability can include water, sugar and nutrient
content, all of which have the ability to dramatically affect many fruit
and vegetable attributes, including flavor, sweetness, texture, weight,
size of seeds, thickness of skin/rind, etc. Keep this in mind when
preparing recipes from this book, which are written with approximate
yields. The amount of water needed to be added to whole foods to
achieve desired purée consistency will vary depending upon the water
content of the batch of produce used. No two apples are ever the same.
No two avocado pits weigh the same. Yields and flavors can vary.

Quality Testing

Save yourself potentially wasted time by *always* tasting your whole foods before puréeing an entire batch, and taste the final purée again before freezing. One rotten piece of produce can ruin the entire batch of purée! Also keep in mind that a batch of puréed apples made from unknowingly tart apples can lead you to believe that baby does not like apples, when really it was just a particularly tart batch. (And, if you end up puréeing an entire batch of overly tart apples, don't toss out the purée. Just pair it with a super sweet fruit, like bananas, to help balance out the flavor profile).

Browning of Fruits and Vegetables

Some fruits and vegetables begin to quickly brown when cut open (apples, bananas, potatoes, avocados, pears, lettuce). These particular fruits and vegetables contain an enzyme (polyphenoloxidase) which, when exposed to oxygen, triggers a process called enzymatic browning. This browning is merely a visual change and does not impact the flavor or indicate spoilage in any way.

There are ways to inhibit enzymatic browning at home (although it is not necessary to do so) which include: blanching produce (place produce in boiling water for 1–2 min), to inactivate the enzyme responsible for catalyzing the browning reaction; refrigerating cut produce, to slow down the rate of the enzymatic reaction; or lowering the pH (increasing the acidity) by rubbing lemon juice on exposed surfaces to prevent the enzyme from functioning.

Skins and Rinds

Some produce have inedible rinds/skins which will always need to be removed and discarded (melons, winter squash, banana peels).

Others have edible skins (apples, pears, potatoes), but some of these skins are not easily digested by baby in the early stages of introducing solid foods. As baby's digestive system matures with an increased and regular consumption of a wide variety of whole foods, eventually plan to prepare produce with their edible skins. These edible skins contain valuable nutrients, and baby will likely be ready to handle digesting them at around 10–12 months. The recipes for these fruits and vegetables are labeled as *Edible skins for later*. If recipes in this book do not indicate peeling as a step in the preparation process, peeling is not necessary at all. If non-organic produce is used, however, consider avoiding skins altogether, in order to limit pesticide exposure.

Cooking Technique

Most babies can handle digesting many raw fruits (no cooking required) by the age of 6 months. Fruits that are fine to prepare without cooking are labeled as *no-cook recipe* in **Chapter 7**. Other fruits, vegetables and legumes require gentle cooking to soften the food, making it more easily digestible by baby.

In order to ensure maximum retention of nutrient and flavor integrity, the most gentle cooking methods are recommended. When cooking is necessary, steaming is the most commonly used method in this book. Roasting is a wonderful alternative for some vegetables, but the process is more time consuming. Whichever method used, always avoid overcooking, which can cause significant nutrient loss. Take care to avoid unnecessary contact of food with water when cooking (do not let water level touch the food being steamed), as water soluble nutrients will readily seep out and be lost in the water. Also take care to not let the water steam completely off when steaming multiple batches of whole foods. Add additional water as necessary during steaming to prevent the steamer from running dry.

When puréeing foods and additional water is needed to smooth out texture, use the cooking water reserved from steaming in order to add back lost nutrients. Do not use the water from steaming, however, if the food is a high-nitrate containing food (see page 174), since this will add back nitrates to your purée. Babies should be able to appropriately digest nitrates that are naturally present in whole foods by 6 months old, but there is no need to unnecessarily add back any nitrates after they are lost. Vegetables that are known to typically have high nitrate levels are labeled as *high nitrates* in their respective recipes.

Microwaving foods is a controversial subject matter. Though regulated by the FDA and regarded as safe for the use of heating and cooking foods when operated correctly, there are many studies indicating both potential health dangers and nutrient loss from foods as a result of microwaving. The use of microwaves in our culture is prevalent, primarily due to convenience. However, as a conservative approach to preserving health and nutrition, I do not encourage the use of microwaves to prepare or re-heat baby food. If you do choose to use the microwave, consider using glass instead of plastic containers for cooking or re-heating food, and take care to avoid hot-spots by stirring food very well before serving to baby.

Using Your Blender or Food Processor

All recipes in this book were developed using a high-speed blender (Vitamix®), but most blenders and food processors will work sufficiently to create the baby food purée recipes presented. One important tip to note about using your machine is that batch size and the size of your blender or processing bowl play an important role in creating smooth purées and finely ground grains. The blade of your machine needs to adequately come into contact with the food being processed. If the processing bowl is too large, the food will not become thoroughly puréed. If you have a particularly large processing bowl, you may need to increase batch sizes to get a smoother purée or finely ground grain. This same concept applies to grinding nuts and seeds, which is why the small size of a coffee grinder works particularly well to grind small quantities (see page 63).

When dry grinding foods (whole grains, lentils, nuts, seeds), it is important to ensure that the blade and mixing bowl are completely dry. For this reason, it is advisable to grind these foods at the beginning of every cooking session, before wetting the mixer components with purées.

Chapter 7

RealSmart Recipes™

All purée recipes have been written to approximately yield quantities to fill one freezer tray, or 15 cubes at 1 fl oz each. For freezing, pour purée into a freezer tray and cover with plastic wrap. Place freezer tray in the freezer for 24 hours, or until completely set, then transfer frozen cubes from the freezer tray into a labeled freezer storage bag.

Refer to this guide when using the following pages

| Peak season | → | Refers to peak season for produce availability |

| *Dirty Dozen Plus™ * | → | This item is part of the Dirty Dozen Plus™ list (page 95) |

| *Clean 15™ * | → | This item is part of the Clean 15™ list (page 95) |

| *Ethylene producer* | → | This item is an ethylene producer (page 98) |

| *Ethylene-sensitive* | → | This item is ethylene-sensitive (page 98) |

| *Available frozen* | → | This item is typically available frozen (page 92) |

| *High nitrates* | → | This item has a naturally high level of nitrates (page 102) |

| *Edible skins for later* | → | This item has skins that should be eaten by baby at a later stage (page 100) |

Fruits

In everyday language, fruits typically refer to the seed-containing fleshy structures of a plant that are sweet and edible in their raw state.

Pome Fruits

Pome fruits are fruits that have a core of several small seeds, surrounded by a tough membrane that is encased in an edible layer of flesh. Pome fruits are members of the plant family *Rosaceae*, sub-family *pomoideae*. Apples and pears are common pome fruits appropriate for baby.

Apples or Pears

Apples or Pears *steamer recipe*
1.5 lb apples or pears (about 4 medium fruits)

Peel fruit and cut into 2 inch chunks, discarding the core. Place in a steamer basket and set in a pot filled with 1–2 inches of simmering water. Cover and steam for 5–7 minutes, until fruit slightly softens and can be pierced easily with a fork. Uncover and remove from heat to let fruit cool down. Reserve cooking liquid.

Place fruit in a blender or food processor and purée, adding reserved cooking liquid, if necessary, until desired consistency is reached (probably close to 1/2 cup).

How to select and store:

Apples

There are more than 7,500 varieties of apples worldwide, many of which are suitable for baby. Avoid apples that are bruised or otherwise visibly damaged. Look for apples that are firm with rich coloring and be sure to choose varieties with low acid levels (not too tart). Suitable varieties include Golden Delicious, Red Delicious, Gala, Fuji, Jonagold, Braeburn... Taste it first. If it tastes sour to you, it's probably too sour for baby.

Apples can be stored for several weeks in the refrigerator.

Peak season: fall	*Ethylene-sensitive*
*Dirty Dozen Plus™ *	*Edible skins for later*
Ethylene producer	

Pears

There are over 3,000 pear varieties worldwide, but the most common and suitable for baby include Bartlett, Anjou, Bosc, Comice and Asian. Bartletts have the highest water content, and are easiest to purée, making them a top choice. Ripeness can be determined by smelling for a strong sweet aroma. Most pears soften as they ripen, but some varieties stay firm. Hold the pear gently but firmly in the palm of your hand, and use your thumb to apply slight pressure to the pear flesh located just below the stem. If the flesh yields evenly to gentle pressure, the pear is ripe and ready to eat.

Pears should be stored at room temperature until ripe. If fully ripe but not yet ready to use, refrigerate pears to suppress further ripening.

Peak season: Each pear variety has its own season, making pears available year round.	*Ethylene producer*
	Ethylene-sensitive
	Edible skins for later

✳ Additional tips:

Due to their high water content, Bartletts will take less time to soften via steaming than other varieties. They may not need to be steamed at all if extremely ripe and soft.

Stone Fruits

Stone fruits (also known as drupe) are fruits that have an outer fleshy part that surrounds a shell (stone/pit) containing a seed. These fruits are of the genus *Prunus*, and include apricots, peaches, nectarines, plums, cherries (and technically also almonds). Many hybrid stone fruits are also becoming increasingly available. There is no need to remove skins from stone fruits before preparing purées for baby.

Peaches, Nectarines, Plums, Apricots, and Hybrid Stone Fruits

Peaches, Nectarines, Plums, Apricots, and Hybrid Stone Fruits *no-cook recipe*
1.5 lb stone fruit

Cut fruit into chunks, discarding pits. Place fruit in a blender or food processor and purée, adding additional water if necessary, until desired consistency is reached (probably 1/4–1/2 cup).

How to select and store:

Store peaches, nectarines, apricots, plums and their hybrid fruits at room temperature until fully ripe. When ripe, these fruits can be stored in the refrigerator for an additional several days.

Peaches

There are 2 categories of peaches: white and yellow (referring to the flesh color inside). Both are delicious when at peak ripeness. Ripe peaches will have a flesh tender to the touch and a classic peachy aroma. Peaches will have varying colors of yellow, red, and orange in their skin (indicating variety, not ripeness), but should never have green coloring (which indicates an underripe fruit). Avoid peaches with tinges of green, or those that are too firm, cracked, bruised or have blemishes.

Peak season: summer	*Ethylene-sensitive*
*Dirty Dozen Plus™ *	*Available frozen*
Ethylene producer	

Nectarines:

Nectarines are a variety of peach, and similar tips apply for selecting ripe fruit. A ripe nectarine will give to gentle pressure, have slight softening on the seam side, and have a fragrant aroma. Avoid greenish color nectarines, or those that are too firm, cracked, bruised or have blemishes.

Peak season: summer	*Ethylene producer*
*Dirty Dozen Plus™ *	*Ethylene-sensitive*

Plums

Plums can range in color from red to purple to black, depending upon the variety. A ripe plum will yield to gentle pressure, especially at the end opposite the stem, and will have a distinct plum aroma. Avoid purchasing plums with skin damage, or plums that are too firm (indicating they were likely harvested too early and will therefore not develop an optimally sweet flavor, even if allowed to ripen further at home).

Peak season: summer–early fall
Ethylene producer
Ethylene-sensitive

Apricots

Apricots are a cousin of the peach, and similar tips apply for selecting ripe fruit. Ripe apricots will have a distinct fragrant aroma. Generally, the deeper its orange color, the riper and sweeter the apricot will be.

Peak season: early summer
Ethylene producer
Ethylene-sensitive

Hybrids *(Pluots, Plumcots, Apriums, Nectarcots, Peacotums, Nectarcotums...)*

Many different stone fruit hybrids now exist and are becoming increasingly available: Pluots (75% plum–25% apricot hybrid), plumcots (50% plum–50% apricot hybrid), apriums (75% apricot–25% plum), nectarcots (nectarine-apricot hybrid), peacotums (peach-apricot-plum hybrid), nectarcotums (nectarine-apricot-plum hybrid), and more. Tips for selecting hybrid fruits are similar to their parent fruits.

Peak season: summer

Ethylene producer

Ethylene-sensitive

Cherries

Cherries *no-cook recipe*
1 lb sweet red or black cherries
(pitting fresh cherries will add additional time to the Real Smart Strategy™ timeline; frozen cherries should be used to avoid adding extra time).

Remove stems and pit cherries, either with a cherry pitter tool (the easiest method), or by cutting cherries in half and removing pits by hand. Place cherries in a blender or food processor and purée until smooth. Additional water will not likely be needed.

How to select and store:

The best way to know if cherries are ripe and sweet is to taste one. Don't be shy about asking to do so when shopping. Cherries should be firm without wrinkling near the stem.

Cherries should be stored in the refrigerator to maintain freshness until ready to purée. Quality will quickly decline when left at room temperature. Avoid washing cherries until ready to purée, as moisture can be absorbed where the stem meets the fruit and lead to early spoilage.

Peak season: summer

Available frozen

· · · · · · · · · · · · · · Tropical and Sub-tropical Fruits · · · · · · · · · · · · · · ·

Tropical and sub-tropical fruits are grown mostly in areas with warm climates within the earth's tropical, sub-tropical and mediterranean zones. The only common characteristic shared among these fruits is their intolerance to frost. Common tropical and sub-tropical fruits appropriate for baby include bananas, avocados, mangoes, papayas, kiwifruit, and figs.

Bananas

Bananas *no-cook recipe*
1.5 lb ripe bananas (about 5 medium bananas)

Peel bananas, then place banana flesh in a blender or food processor and purée until smooth. No additional water needed.

How to select and store:

There are over 1,000 varieties of bananas worldwide, but more than 95% of those sold in the U.S. are of the Cavendish variety. Cavendish bananas will range in color from green to yellow, to turning brown. Ripe bananas will be yellow with or without brown spots, and underripe bananas will be greenish. Bananas should be firm, bright, and the peel should not be crushed or cut. Stems and tips should be intact. Quality of the Cavendish banana is not affected by its size. Other varieties of bananas can be used, but be sure to check the flavor profile before feeding to baby. Also note that although plantains are a banana variety, they must be cooked and rarely reach the sweetness level of a Cavendish.

Bananas are fragile and should be stored at room temperature until the ripening process is complete. Slow down banana ripening of very ripe bananas by placing in the refrigerator. Outer skins will continue to significantly brown, but inner fruit will not. Beware that refrigerating bananas irreversibly halts ripening, so only refrigerate fully ripe bananas.

Peak season: winter-spring (though available year round)

Ethylene producer

Ethylene-sensitive

Bananas can also be very easily prepared for baby by simply mashing with a fork and serving, with no processing required (although, during the initial stages of introducing solid foods you will need to make sure there are no lumps, or baby may reject the texture). A perfect on-the-go food if you find yourself out and about with baby and no prepared food on-hand.

Avocados

Avocados *no-cook recipe*
1.5 lb avocados (about 3 medium avocados)

Cut avocados in half lengthwise and remove seed. Scoop out the green and yellow avocado flesh, discarding the outer skin. Place flesh directly in a blender or food processor and purée until smooth. No additional water needed.

How to select and store:

Although there are almost 500 different varieties of avocados, Hass avocados are the most common. Hass avocados can change from a dark-green color to a deep purple-black color when ripe. To check for ripeness, hold the avocado in the palm of your hand. Without using fingertips (to avoid bruising), gently squeeze the avocado. If it yields to firm gentle pressure, the avocado is ripe and ready to eat. If the avocado does not yield to gentle pressure it will be ripe in a couple of days. If the avocado feels mushy or very soft to the touch it may be overripe. Skin should be tight with no visible spotting, which can indicate infection or bruising. Smell the avocados. They should not have any aroma. If they have a fermented odor, they are no good. One avocado with even slight fermentation will ruin your entire purée batch.

Store avocados at room temperature until fully ripe. Fully ripe avocados that you are not ready to use can be stored in the refrigerator for up to 3 additional days.

Peak season: summer (California), winter (Florida), fall (Imported)	*Clean 15™ *
	Ethylene producer
	Ethylene-sensitive

✳ Additional tips:

• Like bananas, avocados are a great on-the-go food eaten raw. Avocados can be very easily prepared for baby by simply mashing with a fork and serving, with no processing required (although, during the initial stages of introducing solid foods you will need to make sure there are no lumps, or baby may reject the texture).

• Avocados are an exceptional fruit, and what I consider to be a staple in any baby's (or adult's) diet. Avocados are very nutrient dense, providing healthy unsaturated fats, as well as a long list of other essential nutrients and phytonutrients. Unless you have a good reason to avoid avocados, this is one whole food to be sure to include as a regular part of baby's diet.

Mangoes

Mangoes *no-cook recipe*
1.5 lb mangoes (about 2 large mangoes)

Remove mango seed. Mangoes have a unique oblong flat seed at the center of the fruit that can be difficult to work around. The simplest approach to remove the seed and peel is the following: Slice off the two "cheeks" on either side of the the mango pit. Then, gently cut horizontal and parallel lines (forming cube shapes) into the flesh of each cheek, taking care not to cut through the skin (see photo on page 85). Use a spoon to scrape out the mango chunks, discarding the outer skin. Scavenge any flesh surrounding the mango pit. Place mango flesh in a blender or food processor and purée until smooth. No additional water should be needed.

How to select and store:

Over 1,000 varieties of mangoes currently exist, any of which can be used for baby food. Ataulfo (Champagne) mangoes are super sweet and creamy (and also have a high flesh to seed ratio), making them an excellent choice for baby if you can find them. Ripeness of mangoes can be determined by smelling and squeezing. A ripe mango will have a full, fruity aroma emitting from the stem end, and be slightly soft to the touch, yielding to gentle pressure. The best flavored fruit have a yellow tinge when ripe, however, color may be red, yellow, green, orange or any combination, depending on variety.

Mangoes will continue to ripen at room temperature, but ripening will be suppressed if refrigerated.

Peak season: spring-summer (Domestic), fall-winter (Imported)	*Clean 15™*
	Ethylene producer
Available frozen	*Ethylene-sensitive*

Papaya

Papaya (Pawpaw) *no-cook recipe*
2 lbs papayas (about 2 medium papayas)

Peel papaya and slice in halve lengthwise. Use a spoon to scoop out and discard seeds from each half. Chop papaya flesh into chunks and place in a blender or food processor and purée until smooth. No additional water should be needed.

How to select and store:

There are many different types of papayas, but the most common papaya type sold in the U.S. is the *solo* papaya from Hawaii. These papayas will have green skin with an orange/red tinge. Ripe papayas will be slightly soft to the touch.

Papayas will continue to ripen when stored at room temperature. Slow down ripening by storing in the refrigerator.

Peak season: summer-fall	✳ Additional tips:
Available frozen	Papayas contain an enzyme (papain) that helps to break down protein, allowing papayas to function well at tenderizing meat and helping with its digestion when paired in the same meal.
Ethylene producer	
Ethylene-sensitive	

Kiwifruit

Kiwifruit (Chinese Gooseberry) *no-cook recipe*
1.25 lb kiwifruit (about 6 kiwifruit)

Cut kiwifruit in half and scoop out the flesh with a spoon, discarding the fuzzy brown skins (seeds are edible and do not need to be removed). Place green kiwifruit flesh in a blender or food processor and purée until smooth. No additional water should be needed.

How to select and store:

Choose kiwifruit with firm, unblemished brown skin. Choose large or small fruit, as size of kiwifruit is not an indicator of flavor. A ripe kiwifruit will give to slight pressure when the outside of the fruit is pressed with your thumb.

Kiwifruit will keep for several days at room temperature and for up to one month in the refrigerator.

Peak season:
fall-winter (Domestic),
spring-summer (Imported)

*Clean 15™ *

Ethylene producer

Ethylene-sensitive

❋ Additional tips:

Kiwifruit contains an enzyme (actinidin) that helps to break down protein, allowing kiwifruit to function well at tenderizing meat and helping with its digestion when paired in the same meal.

Figs

Figs *no-cook recipe*
1 lb figs

Remove stems, place figs in a blender or food processor and purée until smooth. No additional water should be needed.

How to select and store:

Figs do not ripen after harvesting, so be sure to choose figs that are fully ripe. Figs should be very soft (but not mushy) and plump, with stems intact, with a rich color and unbroken skin. Ripe figs should have a nice sweet aroma. If there is even the slightest fermented odor, the figs are no good. There are several different varieties of figs, and color and flavor profile will be dependent upon variety. Black Mission figs are one of the sweetest varieties, making them an excellent choice for baby. Black Mission figs have dark purple skins and a light pink colored flesh.

Fresh figs are one of the most perishable fruits, and will usually only keep for 1-2 days in the refrigerator after purchasing. It is best to get figs directly from a farmer to limit time between harvest and time of purchase.

Peak season: late summer   ***Ethylene-sensitive***

Ethylene producer

✳ Additional tips:

Figs contains an enzyme (ficin) that helps to break down protein, allowing figs to function well at tenderizing meat and helping with its digestion when paired in the same meal.

Berries

Technically, the botanical definition of a berry is a fleshy fruit having seeds and pulp produced from a single ovary. This definition encompasses a rather large list of fruits, yet does not include many of the common berries that we typically refer to in culinary language. For the purposes of this book I will refer to *berries* as the common berries most of us refer to when using the term (blueberries, raspberries, blackberries, strawberries). The tiny seeds found in berries are all edible. Prepare all berries the same way.

Blueberries, Raspberries, Blackberries, Strawberries

Blueberries, Raspberries, Blackberries, Strawberries
no-cook recipe
1 pint (16 oz) Berries

Remove any stems, place berries in a blender or food processor and purée until smooth. Add additional water, if necessary, until desired consistency is reached.

How to select and store:

Most berries will not continue to ripen after pulling from the vine, so avoid purchasing underripe berries. Store all fresh berries in the refrigerator and wash just before use, not ahead of time or they will deteriorate faster.

Blueberries

There are 2 main types of blueberries sold in the U.S., including cultivated (high-bush) and wild (low-bush), both of which are fine for baby. Ripe blueberries should have a deep blue color, and skins should have a white sheen called a "bloom" which is a sign of freshness. Berries should be firm, dry, plump, with smooth skins. Check for any signs of mold, and if present, choose a different batch.

Peak season: summer

*Dirty Dozen Plus™ *

Available frozen

Raspberries

Fresh raspberries are extremely fragile and perishable. They should be purchased only 1–2 days prior to use. Choose berries that are plump, firm, with a vibrant red color. Avoid berries that are mushy or moldy, or those in a container with any water at the bottom, which are all signs of spoilage.

Peak season: mid-summer–early fall

Available frozen

Blackberries

Like raspberries, blackberries are extremely fragile and perishable. Select and store blackberries as you would raspberries, with the exception of looking for a uniform black/dark purple color.

Peak season: summer

Available frozen

Strawberries

Select strawberries that are dry with a bright, deep red color, glossy appearance, with fresh green caps, stems and leaves. Avoid strawberries that have turned dull or bluish, or those that have started leaking fluid.

Peak season: spring (California and Florida); mid-June to early July (most local strawberries in other parts of North America).

*Dirty Dozen Plus™ *

Available frozen

✳ Additional tips:

• The easiest way to hull strawberries (remove their stems) is to slide a straw through the center from bottom to top, which cleanly lifts out the green calyx.

• Strawberries are a highly acidic fruit, which may cause food sensitivities in some babies (common manifestations include severe diaper rash and other skin inflammation).

Melons

Melons actually belong to the same gourd family as squashes, but they are sweeter, juicer, and treated as fruits. Most melons have a hard outer shell, thick flesh, with a seed-filled midsection on the inside. Common melons suitable for baby include watermelon, cantaloupe and honeydew melon. Whole melons will typically be larger than needed to meet the recipe yields below. Refrigerate remaining melon for later consumption. All melons have a high water content, which will result in a very thin purée.

Watermelon

Watermelon *no-cook recipe*
1 small seedless whole watermelon
(use 2.5 cups cubed watermelon flesh)

Cut watermelon in half through the center, and cut one half into sections. Remove watermelon flesh from the rind, discarding rind and adjacent white flesh. Chop 2.5 cups of red watermelon fruit cubes, place in a blender or food processor and purée until smooth. Additional water will not be needed.

How to select and store:

Ripe watermelons will be firm, dense, evenly shaped, and have a deep-pitched tone when slapped with the bottom of your palm. Avoid watermelons that are partially white or pale green (underripe), have soft spots or feel soft overall, or have any leaking fluid. Yellow color on one side of the watermelon is where the fruit was in contact with the ground and is not an indication of quality or ripeness.

Whole watermelons store well on the kitchen counter or can be refrigerated for up to 3 weeks.

Peak season: summer   *Ethylene-sensitive*

*Clean 15™ *

* Additional tips:

Seedless watermelons are not completely seedless, and usually contain some small white seeds. The blender or food processor can effectively grind down these edible seeds, but you may want to inspect purée for remaining seeds and remove before freezing into purée cubes.

Cantaloupe or Honeydew Melon

Cantaloupe or Honeydew Melon *no-cook recipe*
1 whole cantaloupe or honeydew melon (use 3 cups cubed melon flesh, or about 1/2 of a whole melon)

Cut the melon in half, then scoop out and discard the seeds in each half. Cut each half into quarters, then run a knife between the flesh and rind to remove the rind and adjacent green layer. Chop 3 cups of melon fruit, place in a blender or food processor and purée until smooth. Additional water will not be needed.

How to select and store:

Whole melons store well on the kitchen counter or can be refrigerated for up to 3 weeks.

Cantaloupe

Ripe cantaloupe will have a fragrant cantaloupe aroma on the stem end of the melon, and the stem end will be slightly soft. There will be large webbing on the skin, and the color will be tinged yellow or orange. A juicy melon will produce a sound of rattling seeds when shaken. White/yellow color on one side of the melon is where the fruit was in contact with the ground and is not an indication of quality or ripeness. Avoid melons that have green coloring or have portions of the stem remaining, indicating they were harvested too early. After harvesting, melons will continue to ripen but sugar content does not increase. Also avoid melons with soft, sunken, or dark spots.

Peak season: summer	*Ethylene producer*
Clean 15™	*Ethylene-sensitive*

Honeydew Melon

Ripe honeydew melon will have a creamy yellow color skin that feels slightly waxy. Large honeydews (around 5 lbs) typically have the best flavor. Honeydews should be firm, with a slight softness at the stem end. Like cantaloupe, a juicy melon can be identified by the rattle of seeds when shaken. Avoid melons that are too firm, too soft, have visual blemishes, or a greenish color.

Peak season: summer

Ethylene producer

Ethylene-sensitive

Dried Fruits

Dried fruits are simply fruits that have been dehydrated. Dried fruits are available year round and are a wonderful option when fresh fruits are not in season. Common dried fruits that are readily available and appropriate for baby include dried plums (prunes), apricots, and figs.

Dried Plums (Prunes), Apricots or Figs

Dried Plums (Prunes), Apricots or Figs *heat/steep recipe*
15 medium dried plums, apricots, or figs (about 0.3 lb)
2 cups water

Bring water to a simmer in a small saucepan, add dried fruit, cover with a lid and turn off heat. Let dried fruit steep 10 minutes, then remove lid and allow the fruit and water to cool. Pour plumped fruit and water into a blender or food processor and purée until smooth.

How to select and store:

When purchasing dried fruits, take care to select fruits with no added sugars or sulfites (which can be labeled as sulfites, metabisulfite, sulfur dioxide). Select pure, dehydrated fruit with no additives. Also be sure to select dried fruits that have already been pitted (seeds have been removed). Dried fruits can be found pre-packaged or in the bulk section of some supermarkets.

Dried fruits can keep for several months when stored in a dry location.

Peak season: all year round

✳ Additional tips:

• Dried plums (prunes) are a natural laxative and should be used in moderation unless trying to alleviate constipation.

• Figs contain an enzyme (ficin) that helps to break down protein, allowing figs to function well at tenderizing meat and helping with its digestion when paired in the same meal.

Vegetables

A vegetable is an edible plant or part of a plant, typically referring to the leaf, stem, or root of a plant, excluding seeds and sweet fruit.

Root Vegetables

These underground grown veggies are particularly tasty when roasted in the oven, but steaming is a much faster method that still produces a flavorful purée. Prepare all of these root vegetables the same way.

Carrots, Parsnips, Beets, Turnips, Sweet Potatoes

Carrots, Parsnips, Beets, Turnips, Sweet Potatoes
steamer recipe
1.25 lbs root vegetables

Peel root vegetables, cut off and discard ends (and leafy greens, if attached). Cut vegetable flesh into 1/2 inch thick slices. Place vegetable slices in a steamer basket and set in a pot filled with 1–2 inches of simmering water. Cover and steam for about 8–10 minutes (carrots, parsnips) or 15 minutes (beets, turnips, sweet potatoes), until vegetables slightly soften and can be pierced easily with a fork. Uncover and remove from heat to let vegetables cool down. Place cooked root vegetables in a blender or food processor and purée, adding fresh water, if necessary, until desired consistency is reached (probably close to 3/4 cup).

How to select and store :

The best place to store root vegetables is in a cool, dry, dark, well ventilated location, like a root cellar, where they can keep for months. If you do not have a root storage cellar, use the storage tips described below. If leafy greens are attached to your root veggies, always remove before storing, to prevent greens from pulling moisture out of the root.

Carrots

Carrots can be found in a range of sizes and colors, including orange, red, yellow, white and purple. Look for a vibrant color and smooth shape. If the greens are still attached they should be bright green and not wilted. Slim young carrots are usually the sweetest. Baby carrots are convenient, but are typically less sweet than thin young carrots. Bagged baby carrots are usually made from full-sized carrots that have been whittled down to their small size. Avoid carrots with green coloring at the stem end, cracks, blemishes, wilted greens, or those that are soft or rubbery.

Store carrots in the refrigerator for up to 3 weeks.

Peak season: fall, winter, spring

Ethylene-sensitive

High nitrates

Parsnips

Parsnips look similar to carrots, but are paler in color, and often sweeter when cooked. The whiter the flesh, the sweeter the parsnip. Choose smaller rather than larger parsnips, which tend to be more woody. As with most root vegetables, parsnips can typically be found year round, but winter and early-spring parsnips are usually the sweetest because more starches have time to turn into sugars while parsnips are frozen underground.

Store parsnips in the refrigerator for up to 3 weeks.

Peak season: winter

High nitrates

Beets

Beets may be found in bunches with their leafy greens still attached, or loose with no leafy greens. Beets are most often a deep garnet red color, but can be found in a wide variety of colors, including red, golden, white, and candy cane striped (chioggia beets). Choose small or medium sized beets which typically have optimal flavor and tenderness. Beet skin should be firm, smooth, with a deep color. Avoid beets that have spots, bruises or soft, wet areas, all of which indicate spoilage.

Beets can be stored in the refrigerator for up to 1 month.

Peak season: summer–fall

High nitrates

✳ Additional tips:

- Be aware that consuming beets may cause a red color to appear in the urine and/or stools of some people, but this is not a cause for concern.
- The leafy greens attached to beets are a highly nutritious part of the vegetable. Rather than discarding these greens, steam or sauté them for a tasty side dish.

Turnips

Turnips are round, similar to beets, and can range in color from white to rose to black. The most common turnips are white with a purplish crown. Choose smaller, young turnips, which are the sweetest. Turnips should be dense and firm, with no soft spots. If leafy greens are still attached, they should be bright green and not wilted.

Turnips can be stored in the refrigerator for up to 1 month.

Peak season: fall–winter

High nitrates

✳ Additional tips:

Like beets, the leafy greens attached to turnips are a highly nutritious part of the vegetable. Steam or sauté these greens for a tasty side dish.

Sweet Potatoes

There are several varieties of sweet potatoes, and all can be used, but the Garnet, Jewel and Beauregard varieties are the most moist. The skin color of these varieties can range from copper orange to red to purple, with a bright to dark orange flesh. Select sweet potatoes that are firm, with no visible signs of decay. Evenly shaped potatoes are easier to cut into uniform sizes for even cooking.

Do no store sweet potatoes in the refrigerator, which can produce hardening and a degraded flavor. As with any kind of potato, store in a cool, dry, well ventilated container, where they can last for up to 1 month.

Peak season: fall-winter	*Ethylene-sensitive*
Clean 15™	*Edible skins for later*

Squash

There are two main categories of squash: summer and winter squash. Both will offer up delicious purées for baby.

Summer Squash

Summer squash are harvested when still immature, leaving their skin tender and edible. Unlike winter squash, there is no need to remove the thin-skins or tiny seeds of these squash before puréeing. Prepare all summer squash the same way.

Popular summer squash varieties include: **Yellow, Pattypan (scallop), Yellow Crookneck, Zucchini (courgette).**

Summer Squash *steamer recipe*
1 lb summer squash

Trim off ends and cut squash into 1/2 inch thick slices. Place in a steamer basket and set in a pot filled with 1–2 inches of simmering water. Cover and steam for about 5–7 minutes, until squash slightly softens and can be pierced easily with a fork. Uncover and remove from heat to let squash cool down. Place cooked squash in a blender or food processor and purée. Additional water will not likely be needed.

How to select and store:

Select squash with brightly colored, shiny, unblemished skin. Make sure squash is firm, particularly at the ends.

Store summer squash in the refrigerator until ready to use.

Peak season: mid-summer–early fall

Ethylene-sensitive

Winter Squash

Winter squash are harvested when mature, after the skins have significantly hardened. Winter squash come in many sizes and shapes, but all have very thick rinds, a hollow inner cavity containing hard seeds, and very dense flesh requiring longer cooking times than summer squash. Rinds and seeds must be removed before eating. Winter squash develop a beautiful nutty flavor when roasted in the oven, but steaming is a faster method of cooking that still produces a flavorful purée. All winter squash can be prepared the same way. (Butternut squash is the only winter squash that can be easily peeled before cooking).

Popular winter squash varieties include: **Butternut Squash, Pumpkin, Acorn Squash, Delicata Squash, Buttercup Squash.**

Winter Squash *steamer recipe*
1.25 lb whole winter squash
(or 3 cups cubed squash flesh)

Butternut squash:

Peel skin with a sharp vegetable peeler. Cut off ends and slice squash in half lengthwise. Scoop out and discard seeds and fibrous strings, then cut flesh into 1-inch chunks. Place chunks in a steamer basket and set in a pot filled with 1-2 inches of simmering water. Cover and steam for 7–10 minutes, until squash slightly softens and can be pierced easily with a fork. Uncover and remove from heat to let squash cool down. Place cooked squash in a blender or food processor and purée until desired consistency is reached. Additional water will not likely be needed.

All other winter squash varieties:

Carefully cut winter squash in half. Scoop out and discard seeds and fibrous strings, then cut each half into quarters. Place quartered pieces in a steamer basket, flesh side down, and set in a pot filled with 2 inches of simmering water. Cover and steam for about 20 minutes, until squash slightly softens and flesh can be pierced easily with a fork. Uncover and remove from heat to let squash cool down. Scoop out squash flesh and discard rinds. Place cooked squash in a blender or food processor and purée until desired consistency is reached. Additional water will not likely be needed.

How to select and store:

Select squash that are dense, with a firm rind, an intact stem (which helps avoid moisture loss), and dull-colored skin. Smooth, shiny skin is an indicator that the squash is not ripe. Avoid squash with bruising, cuts, or brown scarring (indicating frostbite), which can degrade quality.

The hard, thick rinds of winter squash allow them to store very well when kept in a dry, cool location. Stored properly, winter squash can keep for 1 month or more.

Peak season: early fall–early winter

Available frozen (butternut squash)

✳ Additional tips:

Fresh winter squash are sometimes available already cut and packaged in the produce section of supermarkets (saving a lot of time and frustration cutting through hard shells).

Super Green Veggies

Green vegetables are nutrition powerhouses. Some babies may take a while to accept the relatively strong flavors of these veggies, but this category is an important part of a well rounded meal plan. Super green veggie purées pair well with fruit purées (bananas, pears, apples), creating a more diluted, sweetened flavor profile that is more easily accepted by baby.

Leafy Greens: Spinach, Kale, Chard

Leafy Greens: Spinach, Kale, Chard *steamer recipe*
1.5 lbs leafy greens (with ribs attached) or
1 lb (16 cups) loose leafy greens (no ribs attached)

Remove large fibrous ribs (thick, central stems), if attached, and discard. To remove ribs, fold leaves in half lengthwise, then tear or slice the stems out with a knife. Stack several leaves together then roughly chop them. Place leafy greens in a steamer basket and set in a pot filled with 1–2 inches of simmering water. You will probably need to work in batches (2–3), depending upon the size of your steamer (leafy greens cook down substantially, which is why the starting quantity of leaves is so large). Cover and steam for 3–5 minutes, gently tossing greens to promote even cooking, until greens wilt. Remove from heat, and repeat with remaining batch(es) if necessary. Place wilted leafy greens in a blender or food processor and purée, adding fresh water, if necessary, until desired consistency is reached (probaby close to 1/2 cup).

How to select and store :

For all leafy greens, look for a deep green, uniform color in the leaves. Avoid greens that have started to turn yellow or brown, or those that have started to wilt. Choose small to medium leaves, which have a milder flavor than larger leaves.

Nutrients of leafy greens degrade with excessive storage time. Do not wash until just before using, as excess moisture will cause leaves to wilt prematurely.

All leafy greens need to be thoroughly cleaned before use because leaves collect soil and debris when growing. The easiest way to clean leafy greens is to place them in a large bowl with room temperature water and stir leaves around to get debris to fall to the bottom. Rinse and repeat until no debris can be seen in the water.

Spinach

Regular or baby spinach can be used, but baby spinach is harvested earlier than regular spinach, resulting in a smaller, more delicate and mildly flavored leaf, making it more ideal for baby food. Baby spinach is readily found both in bulk and pre-packaged in the produce section of most supermarkets, with no ribs to remove.

Spinach should be stored in the refrigerator and consumed within 3–5 days.

Peak season: spring and fall	*Ethylene-sensitive*
*Dirty Dozen Plus™ *	*High nitrates*
Available frozen	

Kale

There are many varieties of kale, but one of the most popular varieties is lacinato kale (also called dinosaur, dino, or Tuscan kale). Lacinato kale has an almost sweet flavor, whereas other varieties have more of a peppery flavor profile. Kale leaves (with ribs already removed) can be found pre-packaged in the produce section of some supermarkets.

Kale is a hearty leafy green, and can last 5–7 days when stored in the refrigerator.

Peak season: winter	*Ethylene-sensitive*
*Dirty Dozen Plus™ *	*High nitrates*

Chard (Swiss Chard; Silverbeet)

The leafy part of chard will always be green, but the stems (which look a lot like celery) can be white, green, yellow, red, pink or orange.

Chard has the shortest shelf-life of the leafy greens. Store chard in the refrigerator for 1-2 days before use.

Peak season: summer	*Ethylene-sensitive*
*Dirty Dozen Plus™ *	*High nitrates*

Broccoli

Broccoli *steamer recipe*
1 lb broccoli florets (not including stalks)

Place broccoli florets in a steamer basket and set in a pot filled with 1-2 inches of simmering water. Cover and steam for 6-8 minutes, until broccoli slightly softens and can be pierced easily with a fork. Broccoli should maintain a bright green color. Remove from heat, remove lid, and let broccoli cool down. Place cooked broccoli in a blender or food processor and purée until desired consistency is reached, adding fresh water if necessary (probably about 1/2 c).

How to select and store:

Choose fresh broccoli with florets that are firm and compact, with an even dark green color. Broccoli that has started to yellow or brown will have an overly strong flavor profile.

Store broccoli in the refrigerator for 3-5 days.

Peak season: fall–spring	*Ethylene-sensitive*
Available frozen	*High nitrates*

✳ Additional tips:

This recipe works the same for **Cauliflower**, **Purple Broccoli** (a cousin of broccoli that looks like small heads of purple cauliflower), and hybrids of broccoli, including **Broccolini** (broccoli-Chinese kale hybrid) and **Broccoflower** (broccoli-cauliflower hybrid).

Asparagus

Asparagus *steamer recipe*
1.5 lb asparagus spears

Snap off and discard woody ends of each asparagus spear (the woody part naturally breaks off at the right point when spear is bent). Place trimmed asparagus in a steamer basket and set in a pot filled with 1–2 inches of simmering water. Cover and steam for 4–8 minutes, depending upon stalk thickness, until the thickest part of asparagus slightly softens and can be pierced easily with a fork. Uncover and remove from heat to let asparagus cool down, reserving cooking liquid. Place asparagus in a blender or food processor and purée, adding reserved cooking liquid, if necessary, until desired consistency is reached.

How to select and store:

Asparagus spears may be chosen thick or thin, but be sure they are fresh, as asparagus loose their sweetness and become woody as they age. Select asparagus spears that have tightly closed tips, and stalks that are vibrant green, straight and firm. A dull green color and ridges in the stems indicate old age. The bottom of the stalks should not be dry.

Do not wash asparagus until just before use. Store asparagus as you would a flower bouquet: trim the ends of fresh spears and stand them upright in a jar with 1-inch water. Store jar in refrigerator for up to 2 days.

Peak season: spring

*Clean 15™ *

Ethylene-sensitive

Legumes

Legumes are a type of pod that opens along a seam. Most legumes are considered to be high-protein containing vegetables.

Fresh Beans and Peas

There are two basic categories of fresh beans: (1) *edible pod beans*, so called because the pod that holds the beans is edible, and (2) *shelled beans*, which are beans that must be removed from their pod before eating since the pod is not edible. Peas can come in edible pods (snow peas, sugar snap peas), or shelled (green garden peas). Whole edible pod peas are not easily digested by baby, but can be introduced as a snack food when baby is older (around 1.5–2 years old).

Edible Pod Beans

Green Beans (snap beans or string beans)
steamer recipe
1 lb green beans

Trim and discard ends of green beans. Place green beans in a steamer basket and set in a pot filled with 1–2 inches of simmering water. Cover and steam for about 5 minutes until green beens can be pierced easily with a fork, maintaining a bright green color. Uncover and remove from heat to let green beans cool down. Place cooked beans in a blender or food processor and purée, adding fresh water if necessary, until desired consistency is reached (probably close to 1/2 cup).

How to Select and Store:

Select fresh beans that are bright green in color, crisp and free of blemishes. Sweeter beans will be slender (no thicker than a pencil). Do not purchase beans that have seeds visible through the pod or those that are too stiff, as these beans will be more fibrous.

Store fresh green beans in the refrigerator, where they can last 4–5 days.

Peak season: late spring–fall

Ethylene-sensitive

*Dirty Dozen Plus™ *

High nitrates

Available frozen

✳ Additional tips:

Haricots Verts (French green beans) are a longer, thinner, more delicate green bean variety that are perfectly suitable for baby. Other edible pod beans suitable for baby include **Yellow Wax Beans**, **Runner Beans**, **Purple Wax Beans**, and **Chinese Long Beans (Asparagus Beans)**. All can be prepared similarly to green beans.

Shelled Beans

Edamame (immature green soybeans) *heat/steep recipe*
1 lb shelled edamame

Place 5 cups water in a medium pot, cover and bring to a simmer. Add edamame and cook for 5 minutes. Drain edamame, reserving cooking liquid. Place cooked edamame in a blender or food processor and purée, adding reserved cooking liquid, if necessary, until desired consistency is reached (probably close to 1/2 cup).

How to Select and Store:

Edamame is rarely sold fresh in the United States, as very few farms are dedicated to producing this type of soybean. If you are lucky enough to find it, fresh edamame should be used within 24 hours of harvesting, so it is best to purchase this legume directly from a farmer. Select edamame with green pods that have not started to yellow. Edamame is readily available frozen year round in two forms: shelled, or in pods. Since pods are inedible, save the trouble and purchase shelled frozen edamame for baby food.

Peak season: mid-August–September

Available frozen

✳ Additional tips:

- Edamame is one of the very few vegetable sources of complete protein (see page 162).

- When baby gets older (around 1.5–2 years old), it will be fun to eat edamame out of the pod as a snack.

Peas (shelled)

Sweet Peas (English Peas) *steamer recipe*

2 lb fresh sweet peas in pods or 1 lb shelled sweet peas

(shelling fresh sweet peas will add additional time to the Real Smart Strategy™ timeline; frozen shelled peas should be used to avoid adding extra time).

Shell peas by removing the stem end of the pod, then peel the fibrous string from the seam, open the pod and run a thumb along the interior, scooping out the peas and discarding pods. Place peas (fresh or frozen) in a steamer basket and set in a pot filled with 1-2 inches of simmering water. Cover and steam for about 2-3 min, until peas turn a bright green color. Remove from heat and let peas cool down, reserving cooking liquid. Place cooked peas in a blender or food processor and purée, adding reserved cooking liquid if necessary, until desired consistency is reached (probably close to 1/2 cup).

How to Select and Store:

When selecting fresh peas, choose smaller pods, which have sweeter and more tender peas than larger pods. Select pods that are firm and green, avoiding those that are yellowing or wilting. To really know if peas are fresh and sweet, break open a pod to look at the peas inside. Peas should be bright green, small and firm. Once the pod is open, taste a pea or two, which should be tender and sweet.

Once peas have been harvested, their sugars immediately start converting to starches, so fresh peas should be used as soon as possible after purchasing for optimal sweetness. Frozen peas will taste better than fresh peas that have been stored too long after harvest and have become too starchy. Store fresh peas in the refrigerator for no more than 2-3 days before using.

Peak season: early spring	*Clean 15™ *
Ethylene-sensitive	*Available frozen*

Dried Beans

Dried beans can be purchased dried or canned (already cooked). Canned beans are nutritionally equivalent to dried beans that are cooked at home, and significantly more convenient. Many bean lovers argue that the texture of home cooked beans far exceeds that found in a can, but since these beans will be puréed for baby, texture of the whole bean really doesn't matter. Recipes for both canned beans and dried beans are provided here, however canned beans should be used to accommodate the timeframe of the *RealSmart Strategy*™. Preparing dried beans at home will require a significant addition of time. Dried beans can generally all be prepared the same way. Common dried beans appropriate for baby include the following:

Pinto Beans, Black Beans, Navy Beans, Kidney Beans, Cannellini Beans (white kidney beans), Garbanzo Beans (chickpeas), Northern Beans

Option 1: Canned Beans (dried beans that have already been cooked) *heat/steep recipe*
Two 15-oz cans of beans
1 cup water

Rinse and drain beans in a colander. Place beans in a medium pot with water, and bring to a simmer over medium heat. Remove from heat and drain beans, reserving cooking liquid. Place beans in a blender or food processor and purée, adding reserved cooking liquid if necessary, until desired consistency is reached (probably about 1/2 cup).

How to select and store:

Look for canned beans with low or no salt added. Also choose beans packed in cans with BPA-free liners, which can be identified by a statement on the label reading "BPA-free Lining."* Always rinse canned beans well before preparing, to remove any sodium that may be present.

Canned beans can be stored for up to 5 years.

*Currently, Eden® Organic is the only brand of canned beans that reliably packs beans in BPA-free lined cans; their beans also have no salt added, and they are cooked with kombu (see footnote page 149).

Option 2: Dried Beans *heat/steep recipe*
1 c dried beans (1/2 lb)
One 1-inch strip kombu[1] (optional)

Sort: before preparing, sort through dried beans, removing those with any blemishes and any debris or pebbles. Place dried beans in a colander and rinse well under cold water.

Soak: soaking not only rehydrates the beans (accelerating cooking time), but it also dissolves gas-producing starches (oligosaccharides) that make bean digestion difficult for some people. Use the following soaking method developed by the California Dry Bean Board to maximize reduction of gas-producing starches:

Place beans in a large pot, cover with water to about 2 inches above the beans. Heat to a simmer, and continue to simmer 2–3 min. Remove from heat, cover, and set aside overnight. The long soaking time allows for more undigestible starches to dissolve. Always discard soaking water before cooking, as this is where all of the dissolved undigestible starches now reside.

Cook: after beans have been soaked and rinsed, place them in a pot and cover beans with 2 inches of fresh water. If you choose to use kombu, add it to the beans now. Bring water to a boil and continue to boil gently, with pot partially covered with a lid (remove lid if foaming becomes a problem). Stir periodically and add water as needed during the cooking process to make sure water level stays above the beans. Beans are ready when they are tender, but still hold their shape (they should mash very

1. Kombu is a little-known sea vegetable that can be optionally added during the cooking process of beans to decrease naturally present gas-producing compounds. Kombu can be found in the Asian section of the supermarket, next to other seaweeds.

easily when gently squeezed with fingers). Exact cooking time depends upon many factors, including age of the beans, water hardness, altitude, and bean variety. Most beans listed here can take anywhere from 1.5–3 hours to cook, depending upon the factors listed above. Remove and discard kombu strip (if using), drain beans and reserve cooking liquid. Place cooked beans in a blender or food processor and purée, adding reserved cooking liquid if necessary, until desired consistency is reached (probably about 1/2 cup).

How to select and store:

The surface of dried beans should be firm, and beans should be uniform in size and color. Avoid any beans that are broken or wrinkled. Dried beans can be purchased pre-packaged or in the bulk section of some supermarkets. Kombu can typically be found in the Asian foods section, next to other seaweeds.

Dried beans can keep for up to 1 year if stored properly. For optimal shelf-life, dried beans should be stored in an airtight container, in a cool, dry location (cabinet, pantry). Beans exposed to high temperatures or humidity may not cook well. Beans that are too old will take longer to cook, or may not soften at all.

Peak season: all year round

Lentils

Lentils are legumes that have been grown in a pod, and then typically dried, like dried beans. Unlike dried beans, lentils do not require soaking, and they cook much faster. Many different varieties of lentils are available, ranging in color from brown to green, yellow, black, and red. Any lentil variety can be used, but the slightly sweet taste of red lentils makes them a favorite for baby. Lentils do not freeze very well, however, so for baby food, I like to grind lentils into a flour, and sometimes pair it with a ground cereal grain to create a *complete protein* cereal (see page 162). Once the flour is ground, small batches of lentil or lentil/grain cereal can then be quickly cooked as needed.

Lentils

Lentil or Lentil/Rice Flour *dry grind recipe*
1 cup dried lentils (1/2 lb) or
1/2 c dried lentils + 1/2 c brown rice

Place lentils (and rice if using) in a blender or food processor and grind into a fine powder. Store in an airtight container at room temperature for up to 1 month, or in the refrigerator for 2–3 months. Use lentil flour to make lentil cereal, described below.

Yields approximately 1 cup (16 T) lentil or lentil/rice flour

Lentil or Lentil/Rice Cereal *heat/steep recipe*
2 T lentil or lentil/rice flour (see recipe above)
1 cup water

In a small pot, bring water to a simmer and slowly add lentil or lentil/rice flour while whisking. Whisk continuously for 5–8 minutes, until think and smooth. Remove from heat and allow cereal to cool. Store in an airtight container in the refrigerator for up to 1 week. Use as needed at meal time (typically starting with 1 tablespoon of cooked lentils at a time).

Yields approximately 3/4 cup (12 T) cooked cereal

How to Select and Store:

Select lentils that are dry, firm, clean, unwrinkled, with uniform coloring. Lentils can be found in the supermarket either pre-packaged next to dried beans, or in the bulk section of some supermarkets.

Whole lentils can be stored for up to one year in an airtight container placed in a dry, cool location.

Peak season: all year round

✳ Additional tips:

Dried **Split Peas** can be prepared and used the same way as lentils.

Whole Grains

Whole grains are the entire seed of a plant, containing the germ, bran and endosperm (as opposed to refined grains which have had the nutrient-rich germ and bran removed and only retain the endosperm).

Whole grains can be easily added to baby's early meals by grinding grains into their respective flours, then creating cooked cereals (porridge) from those flours. High-speed blenders, such as the Vitamix®, easily grind whole grains into flours. Most other blenders and food processors can get the job done as well, but be sure to check your owner's manual beforehand.

Any grain can be used for baby food, though the most common grain to begin with is rice. Gluten-containing grains* should be reserved for a later stage (around 10 months old) because they are more difficult to digest. Common whole grains suitable for baby food cereals include: **Brown Rice, Oats** (whole groats, steel cut or rolled)**, Quinoa, Buckwheat, Millet, Barley*** and **Kamut®***. Prepare all of these whole grain flours and cereals using the same recipe shown for brown rice below, noting that yields will vary slightly depending on grain size and the individual grain's water holding capacity.

Brown Rice Flour *dry grind recipe*
1 cup brown rice grains (1/2 lb)

Place brown rice grains in a blender or food processor and grind into a fine powder. The time it takes to grind whole grains into a fine flour can range from 1 minute (Vitamix®) to 5 minutes, depending upon the motor strength of the individual blender or food processor used. Store flour in an airtight container until ready to use for preparing brown rice cereal (see recipe below).

Yields approximately 1 cup (16 T) brown rice flour

Brown Rice Cereal *heat/steep recipe*
2 T brown rice flour (see recipe above)
1 cup water

In a small pot, bring water to a simmer and slowly add rice flour while whisking. Whisk continuously for 5–8 minutes, until all water is absorbed and cereal is think and smooth. Remove from heat and allow cereal to cool. Store in an airtight container in the refrigerator for up to 1 week. Use as needed at meal time (typically starting with 1 tablespoon of cooked cereal at a time). When serving, adjust prepared cereal consistency as needed, adding water, breast milk or formula to thin out the texture if necessary.

Yields approximately 3/4 cup (12 T) cooked brown rice cereal

How to Select and Store:

Whole grains (unlike refined grains) retain the germ portion of their kernel, which contains many nutritious oils. During prolonged storage, these oils have a tendency to oxidize (react with oxygen to form rancid, off flavors), and heat, light and air accelerate that process. Whole grains are available pre-packaged as well as in bulk containers at many supermarkets. If purchasing pre-packaged whole grains, always check to see if there is a "use-by date." If purchasing from bulk containers, smell the grains from the container, which should smell slightly sweet or have no odor at all. If the grains smell moldy, or like rancid oil, they are no longer good.

Most whole grains can be stored in their unopened package or in an airtight container for several months at room temperature in a dark, dry location (pantry or cupboard), or up to 1 year in the freezer. Once ground into a flour, the natural oils from the whole grain germ are more susceptible to oxidation, so flours should be stored in an airtight container in a refrigerator or freezer to prevent oxidation from occurring. Most whole grain flours will keep for up to 2–3 months in the refrigerator or up to 6–8 months in the freezer.

Cooked whole grain cereals do not freeze well, and it is recommended to instead prepare batches on a weekly basis and store in the refrigerator (where cereals can last up to 1 week), to be used as needed for baby's meals.

Peak season: all year round

✱ Additional tips: . . . .

• Whole grain flours can also be combined with lentil or split pea flour to form a *complete protein* cereal (see **Lentils recipe**). Quinoa is the only whole grain providing a source of complete protein (page 162).

• For the older baby, refer to page 67 for preparation guidelines of whole grains in their unground form.

Bonus Chapters

1. All About Nutrients

Nutrients are substances needed for growth, metabolism, and other body functions. It is important to point out that while understanding detailed information regarding specific nutrients can be helpful toward creating a balanced diet, *it is far more beneficial to focus on offering a wide variety of whole foods rather than meticulously calculating amounts of individual nutrients consumed* (unless advised by your pediatrician to do so, due to specific health concerns). This section provides a detailed discussion of nutrients, offering information for a better understanding of how food components affect general human health, as well as identifying known natural food sources of specific nutrients.

Macronutrients

Macronutrients are nutrients that our bodies need in large amounts, and are responsible for providing energy (calories). Macronutrients include carbohydrates, proteins and fats.

Carbohydrates

Carbohydrates are the main source of fuel for the human body, and they are the most easily digested and utilized source of energy. Carbohydrates are needed for the proper functioning of many parts of the body, including the brain, central nervous system, muscles, and kidneys. They are also important for waste elimination and maintaining intestinal health.

Simple vs. Complex
Carbohydrates are classified as simple or complex, with the classification depending on the chemical structure of the specific

carbohydrate and how quickly the carbohydrate is digested and absorbed. Carbohydrates are chains of sugars. *Simple carbohydrates* have one or two sugars in their chain, while *complex carbohydrates* have three or more sugars. Simple carbohydrates are generally "sweet" and are digested and absorbed relatively fast, providing quick energy. Complex carbohydrates are often referred to as "starchy", and take much longer for digestion and absorption to occur, providing a more gradual release of energy.

Simple carbohydrates such as glucose, fructose, sucrose and lactose, occur naturally in fruits, vegetables and dairy products, and accompany important vitamins and minerals when eaten in their whole food form. Simple carbohydrates, in the form of added sugars, are prevalent in many processed and refined foods, including but not limited to sweetened beverages, candy, syrups, table sugar and packaged snacks. These refined added sugars are often called "empty calories" because they lack vitamins, minerals and fiber. High fructose corn syrup (a syrup derived from corn that has undergone enzymatic processing to increase sweetness by converting some of its glucose into fructose) is a prevalent refined sugar used to sweeten many processed foods. The U.S. food industry began replacing sucrose (table sugar derived from sugar cane or beets) with the cheaper high fructose corn syrup in the 1970's, and it has been using it ubiquitously ever since, despite its correlations with increased risk of obesity, cardiovascular disease, diabetes, and liver disease. Due to their "emptiness" and potential correlation to health risks, all added refined sugars should play a very limited part in a balanced diet.

Complex carbohydrates occur naturally in legumes (beans, lentils, peanuts, peas), starchy vegetables, and whole grains, and accompany important vitamins and minerals when eaten in their whole food form. Many refined foods, including white flour and white rice, have been stripped of many of these vitamins and minerals (although they may be fortified post-processing; these refined grains are referred to as "enriched"). In order to maximize nutrients provided, foods in their most natural, unrefined form are the healthiest option.

Fiber

Fiber is a specific type of carbohydrate found in natural plant-based foods that our bodies cannot digest (it does not break down in the stomach). There are two main types of fiber: *soluble* and *insoluble*, and both are important for health and digestion, though their functions are slightly different. Soluble fiber absorbs water, while insoluble fiber does not. The water absorbing capacity of soluble fiber causes digestion to slow down, and the stomach to feel more full. Since soluble fiber absorbs water, high soluble fiber diets must be accompanied by enough water to prevent constipation. Since breast milk is largely composed of water, additional water is not typically needed in significant amounts for breastfed infants, as long as breast milk remains a substantial part of the diet. Insoluble fiber, on the other hand, does not absorb water, and this type of "bulky" fiber moves rapidly though the digestive system, speeding up the passage of food and waste in the intestinal tract, having a laxative effect. Both types of fiber are equally important for health and digestion. Adequate dietary fiber is essential for intestinal health, and has also been shown to decrease the risk for diet-related diseases such as coronary heart disease, high cholesterol and obesity.

*Soluble fiber: oats, legumes, nuts, seeds, fleshy fruits (apples, oranges, pears, berries, plums), some vegetables (broccoli, carrots, sweet potatoes, onions).

*Insoluble fiber: whole grains, legumes, nuts, seeds, some vegetables (zucchini, celery, broccoli, cauliflower, green beans, dark leafy vegetables), many fruit and vegetable skins (sweet potatoes, white potatoes, tomatoes, kiwifruit, grapes/raisins, plums/prunes), avocados, bananas.

Protein

Proteins are an important source of energy for growth, tissue repair, immune function, making essential hormones and enzymes, and preserving lean muscle mass. Protein takes longer to digest than carbohydrates, and therefore does not provide energy as rapidly. Protein consumption results in increased satiety as compared to consuming carbohydrates alone, allowing the body to get full faster, and stay full longer.

Proteins are made from building blocks called amino acids. There are 20 different amino acids that we consume from food, 9 of which are considered *essential* because they are not made by the human body (the remaining 11 amino acids are referred to as *non-essential* because the body has the ability to synthesize them).

Essential Amino Acids		Non-Essential Amino Acids	
Histidine	Phenylalanine	Alanine	Cysteine
Isoleucine	Threonine	Aspartic Acid	Glutamine
Leucine	Tryptophan	Asparagine	Glycine
Lysine	Valine	Glutamic Acid	Proline
Methionine		Serine	Tyrosine
		Arginine	

Complete and Incomplete Proteins:

A *complete protein* (high quality protein) is a protein source that contains all 9 essential amino acids. Complete proteins come from animal-based products (meat, dairy, eggs), and very few vegetable sources, including soy beans and quinoa. An *incomplete protein* (lower quality protein) either contains fewer than all 9 essential amino acids, or has one or more essential amino acids in insufficient quantities. Most vegetable sources of protein are incomplete. However, complementary incomplete protein sources can be combined during meals, or over the course of a day, to cumulatively provide all necessary amino acids. By consuming a wide variety of plant foods, all essential amino acids can be supplied. Example combinations include rice and beans, corn and beans, peanut butter and wheat toast.

> ✳ **Natural Food Sources**
>
> *Complete proteins: meat (beef, poultry, lamb, fish), dairy products (cheeses, yogurts, kefir), eggs, soybeans (edamame), quinoa.
> *Incomplete proteins: (1) legumes (beans, lentils, peas, peanuts), (2) whole grains, (3) nuts and seeds. Combine any two of the above categories of incomplete proteins to provide all essential amino acids.

Fat

Fat is the most concentrated source of macronutrient energy, (1 gram of fat provides 9 calories, while 1 gram of carbohydrate or protein provides 4 calories), and it is digested more slowly than carbohydrates and proteins, resulting in increased satiety. Fat is essential for normal growth and development, providing cushioning for organs, maintaining cell membranes, and for absorbing fat soluble vitamins from foods. All types of fats, with the exception of trans fats (which are mostly man-made), play individual roles as important nutrient sources. Fats are an especially important source of calories and nutrients for infants and toddlers. *Do not restrict the intake of dietary fat and calories during the first 2 years of life,* particularly when fat is obtained from natural sources. Infants and toddlers specifically need calories and components from dietary fat for their brains and bodies to grow and mature normally during the early months and years of life. Remember: *FaT CaN be healthy!*

Saturated, Unsaturated, and Trans Fats

There are three main types of dietary fat: saturated fat, unsaturated fat, and trans fat. Foods never contain only one type of fat, but rather some combination thereof. Each type of fat refers to its chemical structure, and the chemical structure is responsible for its physical functions. Foods rich in saturated fats tend to be solid at room temperature and have a higher melting point (e.g. butter), while foods rich in unsaturated fats tend to be liquid at room temperature and have a lower melting point (e.g. olive oil). Man-made trans fats result from the commercial process of hydrogenation, which chemically alters unsaturated fats (in the effort to make them more stable), changing their typical room temperature form from liquid-like to more solid like (e.g. stick margarine).

Saturated fats are mainly found from animal sources, including meats, dairy products, butter and lard. There are also plant sources of saturated fats, including coconut oil, palm kernel oil, and cocoa butter. Saturated fat is typically regarded as "bad fat," due to its links to high cholesterol, cardiovascular disease and stroke. Naturally sourced saturated fat in moderation and as part of a balanced diet, however, can be an important supply of energy, particularly when from plant sources.

Unsaturated fats are widely found in fish, nuts and seeds (and their extracted oils), and some grass-fed meats. Unsaturated fats are typically regarded as "good fats," due to their links in reduction of cardiovascular disease, improved blood sugar control, decreased blood pressure, and increases in HDL ("good") cholesterol. *Essential fatty acids* are specific unsaturated fats that are not synthesized by humans but are required by the body to be healthy. There are two main classes of essential fatty acids: *omega-3* and *omega-6*. These two classes of essential fatty acids produce hormones in the body that generally have opposing effects. Omega-6 fatty acids are the building blocks for hormones that tend to increase inflammation, blood clotting and cell proliferation, while those of omega-3 fatty acids act to decrease these functions. Omega-3 fatty acids create hormones that control blood clotting, immune function, cell growth, the components of cell membranes, and play an important role in decreasing inflammation throughout the body. A balance of both classes of hormones is necessary to maintain optimal health and homeostasis. Typical Western diets tend to be much higher in omega-6 fatty acids than omega-3 fatty acids, which is believed by many to have detrimental health effects and play a role in many chronic diseases. Soybean oil is particularly high in omega-6 fatty acids, and since it is used ubiquitously in processed foods, soybean oil accounts for a large portion of omega-6 fatty acid consumption in Western diets. A large body of evidence suggests that increasing the relative abundance of dietary omega-3 fatty acids may have numerous health benefits, including boosting heart health, and lowering blood triglycerides.

✳ Natural Food Sources

*Unsaturated fats:

Avocados, olives, peanuts, tree nuts (almonds, cashews, macadamia nuts, hazelnuts, pecans), seeds (pumpkin, sesame, sunflower, flax, hemp, chia), soybeans, corn oil, fish, grass-fed meats.

✳ Natural Food Sources

*Omega-3 fatty acids:

Walnuts, ground flaxseed, hempseed, dark green leafy vegetables, seaweed, cold water fish (including wild salmon, herring, sardines, black cod, and bluefish), grass-fed meats, specialty eggs (typically from chickens fed flaxseed or seaweed).

✳ Natural Food Sources

*Omega-6 fatty acids:

Vegetable and seed oils (corn, soybean, sunflower, safflower), animal meats.

Trans fats are regarded as "very bad" fats, and they are found in many processed foods, including packaged snack foods, commercially baked goods, vegetable shortening, stick margarine, and fried foods. Trans fats also exist very minimally in nature (found in very small quantities in meat and dairy products), but these natural sources do not account for any significant portion of trans fat in the diet. Trans fats have been shown to have detrimental health effects, including an increased risk of cardiovascular disease, an increase in LDL ("bad") cholesterol and a decrease in HDL ("good") cholesterol. Significant effort has been put forth toward limiting trans fats from processed foods, but they still exist in many food products.

Micronutrients

Micronutrients are nutrients that our bodies need in smaller amounts, and include vitamins and minerals.

Vitamins are organic compounds required by the human body for maintaining health. Vitamins have many roles, including to help release energy from foods, develop red blood cells, help in blood clotting, and help maintain healthy eyes, skin, hair and other organs in the body. Minerals help with the formation of bones and teeth, blood coagulation, muscle contraction, and balancing blood pH levels. While all vitamins, A, Bs, C, D, E and K , are essential for the body, all minerals are not. Some important minerals for the body include, but are not limited to, calcium, iron, sodium, magnesium, potassium, iodine, selenium, zinc, phosphorous.

It is best to consume vitamins and minerals from a variety of natural food sources rather than supplements. Nutrients are generally more bio-available (easily absorbed and assimilated by the body) when consumed from natural food sources. Additionally, many supplements may contain nutrients in excessive quantities. Consuming too much of certain vitamins and minerals can be just as detrimental as consuming too little. Generally, if a wide variety of whole foods are consumed as part of a balanced diet, all vitamin and mineral needs will be easily met.

Fat Soluble Vitamins: A, D, E and K

In order for fat soluble vitamins to be absorbed and utilized by the body, adequate dietary fat intake must occur. Remember: *FaT CaN be healthy!* Fat soluble vitamins do not need to be consumed every day because they are stored in the liver and fatty tissues of the body, and they are eliminated at a relatively slow rate. Since fat soluble vitamins are stored in the body for long periods of time, they can pose a risk for toxicity if consumed in excess. Eating a well balanced diet of natural whole foods will not lead to toxicity in otherwise healthy individuals, however taking dietary supplements with large doses of fat soluble vitamins may lead to toxicity.

Vitamin A

Vitamin A can be obtained in 2 main forms from foods: (1) *preformed vitamin A*, from animal sources, and (2) *beta-carotene* (also called provitamin A), from plant sources, which the body converts to retinol (a form of vitamin A). Vitamin A is essential for normal growth, bone development, vision, reproductive health, and healthy skin. Beta-carotene, specifically, also functions as an antioxidant.

✳ **Natural Food Sources** ·

*Preformed vitamin A (animal sources): Full-fat and low-fat dairy products, animal fat, liver, fish oils, egg yolks.

*Beta-carotene (plant sources): orange/red vegetables and fruits (carrots, sweet potatoes, mangoes, apricots, cantaloupe), dark leafy green vegetables.

Vitamin D

The main role of vitamin D is to promote absorption of calcium and to help maintain healthy blood levels of calcium and phosphorus, all of which are important for the development and maintenance of healthy bones and teeth. The naturally occurring form of vitamin D is known as vitamin D3, or cholecalciferol. Vitamin D2, a form of vitamin D found in many dietary supplements, is a much less effective form of vitamin D.

When adequate sunlight (specifically, Ultraviolet B radiation) is received, the human body has the ability to synthesize sufficient amounts of vitamin D (in the form of vitamin D3) to meet nutritional needs. The factors that affect sunlight exposure, such as season, time of day, sunscreen usage, skin melanin content, cloud cover, smog, and geographic latitude, make it difficult to set guidelines for receiving adequate exposure for vitamin D synthesis. Adequate sunlight has been defined by some researchers as at least 10–30 minutes of sunlight exposure to the face, arms, legs or back, without sunscreen, at least twice per week, between the hours of 10am–3pm. Although sun exposure is important for natural vitamin D synthesis, excessive exposure to sunlight should be limited to avoid increased risk of skin cancer[1,2,3].

1. Holick MF. Vitamin D deficiency. N Engl J Med 2007; 357:266-81.
2. Holick MF. Vitamin D: the underappreciated D-lightful hormone that is important for skeletal and cellular health. Curr Opin Endocrinol Diabetes 2002; 9:87-98.
3. Institute of Medicine, Food and Nutrition Board. Dietary Reference Intakes for Calcium and Vitamin D. Washington, DC: National Academy Press, 2010.

Vitamin E

Vitamin E is the major fat soluble antioxidant of the body, preventing oxidation and the propagation of free radicals. Vitamin E protects red blood cells and prevents destruction of vitamin A and vitamin C. Vitamin E also functions in cell signaling, gene expression, and regulation of other cell functions.

Vitamin K

Vitamin K is necessary in the body for normal blood clotting and for synthesis of proteins found in bones, kidneys, and blood. There are two naturally occurring forms of vitamin K: *vitamin K1* (phylloquinone), the most predominant form in the diet, found in plants, and *vitamin K2* (menaquinone), found in much smaller quantities from animal sources. Vitamin K2 is also synthesized by bacteria in the human intestines. Intestinal bacteria actually synthesize a significant portion of the vitamin K requirements for the human body. One reason why newborns are given a vitamin K injection shortly after birth is to give them a short term supply of the vitamin until their intestines become colonized with enough bacteria to produce it for themselves. Prolonged use of antibiotics can lead to vitamin K deficiency because antibiotics destroy the vitamin K-producing bacteria.

Water Soluble Vitamins (Bs and C)

Unlike fat soluble vitamins, water soluble vitamins are not stored in the body, and therefore need to be regularly consumed. Excess intake of water soluble vitamins will be readily excreted in the urine. For this reason, water soluble vitamins are also much less likely to pose a risk of toxicity if consumed in high quantities.

Vitamin Bs

There are a total of eight B vitamins, all of which play important, unique roles in cell metabolism. B vitamins include: B1 (thiamine), B2 (riboflavin), B3 (niacin), B5 (pantothenic acid), B6 (pyridoxine), B7 (biotin), B9 (folic acid), and B12 (cobalamin). B vitamins are fairly ubiquitous throughout the categories of whole foods, with several B vitamins usually coexisting together within any given food. Vitamin B12, however, is only naturally found in animal products, making vitamin B12 deficiency a major concern with vegan diets.

min C

amin C is needed for the formation of collagen, a protein used to make skin, tendons, ligaments and blood vessels. Vitamin C helps to heal wounds and form scar tissue, repair and maintain cartilage, bones and teeth, and boost the immune system. Vitamin C also functions as a major antioxidant that works to prevent damage caused by free radicals.

> ✳ **Natural Food Sources** . . . .
>
> *Vitamin C: citrus fruits, strawberries, kiwifruit, mangoes, papaya, cantaloupe, pineapple, red and green sweet bell peppers, tomatoes, leafy greens (spinach, kale, chard), Brussels sprouts, broccoli, cauliflower, turnips.

Notable Minerals

Iron

Iron functions primarily as a carrier of oxygen in the body. Iron deficiency anemia occurs when there is not enough iron available in the red blood cells. Infants are born with iron stores that are sufficient to nourish them for the first 6 months of life. After 6 months, iron stores are typically depleted and baby must consume iron from external food sources. Iron deficiency is the most common nutritional deficiency among babies, and can have symptoms including paleness, and a general feeling of weakness and fatigue.

Iron is naturally available from both animal and plant based foods, and is referred to as *heme iron* and *non-heme iron*, respectively. Heme iron is only found in meats and is much more readily absorbed than non-heme iron from plant sources. When relying on non-heme sources for iron, pairing the iron source with a vitamin C-rich food will greatly enhance iron absorption when consumed together at the same meal. Conversely, pairing a non-heme iron source with a calcium-rich food (such as dairy products) at the same meal, will inhibit iron absorption.

✳ Natural Food Sources

*Heme iron: meats (particularly dark), including beef, poultry, pork, lamb, fish.

*Non-heme iron: beans, lentils, spinach, nuts, seeds, dried fruits (apricot, prune, dates, raisins), soybeans, blackstrap molasses.

Calcium

Calcium functions to build bones and teeth, and is also needed for muscle, heart and digestive health. Breast milk or formula typically provide all of the calcium that baby needs. When breast milk or formula consumption significantly declines, usually by baby's first birthday, food sources of calcium should be included in baby's diet.

✳ Natural Food Sources

*Calcium: dairy products, eggs, nuts, seeds (especially sesame), dark green leafy vegetables, soybeans, seaweed.

	Fruits	Veggies	Legumes	Whole Grains	Nuts	Seeds	Eggs	Dairy	Fish	Meat
Phytonutrients	✓	✓	✓	✓	✓	✓				
Complete Protein			✓ edamame	✓ quinoa			✓	✓	✓	✓
Incomplete Protein			✓	✓	✓	✓				
Simple Carbohydrates	✓	✓						✓		
Complex Carbohydrates		✓	✓	✓	✓	✓				
Fiber	✓	✓	✓	✓	✓	✓				
Unsaturated Fat	✓ avocado				✓	✓	✓	✓	✓	✓
Omega-3 Fat		✓ leafy greens			✓	✓	✓ specialty		✓ cold-water	✓ grass-fed
Saturated Fat							✓	✓		✓
Vitamin A	✓	✓					✓	✓		
Vitamin D							✓	✓ fortified	✓	✓
Vitamin E	✓ avocado	✓			✓	✓	✓	✓		
Vitamin K		✓	✓		✓	✓				
Vitamin C	✓	✓								
Vitamin Bs	✓	✓	✓	✓	✓	✓	✓	✓	✓	✓
Vitamin B12							✓	✓	✓	✓
Heme Iron									✓	✓
Non-Heme Iron	✓	✓	✓	✓	✓	✓	✓			
Calcium	✓	✓	✓		✓	✓	✓	✓	✓	

Whole food categories and the *major* nutrients they provide. This chart was compiled through analyzing data of individual whole foods using the USDA National Nutrient Database. Minerals analyzed here are limited to iron and calcium. Nutrients primarily found only in specific foods within a food category are indicated.

2. Nitrates

Nitrates are a natural component of plants and nitrate-containing fertilizers which aid in the growth of fruits and vegetables. Vegetables contain varying levels of nitrates depending upon many factors, including vegetable type, the environment they are grown in, and how they are stored and processed. In addition to being present in some vegetables, nitrates also often seep into well water.

When nitrates are digested, they can be particularly harmful to infants younger than 6 months of age. Prior to the age of 6 months, infants have an insufficient level of stomach acid, which allows the rapid conversion of nitrates into nitrites. Nitrites react with hemoglobin in the blood, forming high amounts of methemoglobin, which can lead to deprivation of oxygen to the blood and vital organs. This can result in nitrate poisoning, or "blue baby syndrome" (methemoglobinemia), so named because baby's skin takes on a blueish tint. This syndrome can be fatal.

Nitrate poisoning is rare. Most cases occur in infants under 6 months of age, and are usually related to the use of contaminated well water to prepare infant formula, rather than the consumption of nitrate-containing vegetables. Nonetheless, it is recommended to not feed high nitrate containing vegetables to infants under 6 months of age. Vegetables that are known to typically have a high nitrate content include *root vegetables (beets, carrots), green beans, spinach, and other dark leafy green vegetables*. These vegetables are labeled in *RealSmart Recipes*™ (**Chapter 7**) as *high nitrates*. Nitrate-containing vegetables should not be feared after the age of 6 months, since baby will have enough stomach acidity at that time to prevent the conversion of nitrates into nitrites.

*Nitrates: root vegetables (beets, carrots), green beans, spinach, and other dark leafy green vegetables.

Use the following tips to limit nitrate exposure:

- If you use well water, it is highly recommended to have it tested for nitrate-nitrogen content (maximum level should be less than 10 ppm (or 10 mg/L)). If well water exceeds this limit, do not use well water to make homemade baby food, formula, or offer it to baby it any form. Use bottled water instead.

- Avoid offering high-nitrate containing vegetables (root vegetables, green beans, spinach, and other leafy greens) until 6 months of age, when baby's digestive system has matured enough for stomach acid levels to increase.

- Limit storage time of nitrate-containing vegetables prior to puréeing and freezing, as nitrates continue to develop during storage (though not in the freezer).

- When preparing baby purées with high-nitrate produce, do not use cooking liquid reserved from steaming to thin out the purée. The cooking liquid will contain concentrated nitrates from the cooked produce. Use fresh water instead.

- Choose organic. Organically grown produce has fewer nitrates than conventionally grown produce due to lack of commercial nitrate-containing fertilizer use during growth.

3. Mercury and Fish

Fish and shellfish provide an excellent source of nutrients, including protein, omega-3 fatty acids, and other essential nutrients. Some fish, however, contain unsafe levels of methylmercury, a form of mercury that can be toxic to humans when consumed at high levels. Nearly all fish and shellfish contain traces of mercury, but some fish and shellfish contain high enough amounts of mercury to harm an unborn baby or young child's developing nervous system. In 2004, the EPA and FDA issued a standing joint federal advisory for mercury in fish, advising women who may be pregnant, pregnant women, nursing mothers, and young children to avoid high-mercury containing fish.

The health benefits of eating fish can and should be enjoyed by choosing fish and shellfish with low mercury levels, while avoiding consumption of high-mercury containing fish.

Mercury is a metal that occurs naturally in the environment. Mercury is also released into the air from industrial pollution. Most mercury pollution in the air then falls directly into waterways or onto land, where it can be washed into different bodies of water. Bacteria in water can change mercury into methylmercury, which is absorbed by small aquatic organisms. When fish feed on these organisms, methylmercury quickly builds up in their muscle tissue. Since big fish, such as shark, swordfish, tilefish and king mackerel, feed on smaller fish, methylmercury is particularly high in the muscle tissue of big fish. Since methylmercury binds to muscle tissue, it cannot be removed by cooking or cleaning the fish.

✳ Natural Food Sources

• AVOID •

Highest mercury level fish and shellfish: shark, swordfish, tilefish, king mackerel, ahi and bigeye tuna, orange roughy, marlin.

• SAFE TO CONSUME •

Lowest mercury level fish and shellfish: shrimp, salmon*, pollock, catfish, canned light tuna, tilapia, crab (domestic), butterfish, haddock, perch (ocean), sole, trout, whitefish, whiting, scallops, squid (calamari), crawfish/crayfish, herring, mullet, sardines, anchovies.

*farmed salmon may contain PCBs (polychlorinated biphenyls), chemicals with serious long-term health effects. Choose wild salmon instead of farmed.

4. Conversion Charts

Liquid/Dry Measures

U.S.	Metric
1 teaspoon	5 milliliters
1 tablespoon (3 teaspoons)	15 milliliters
1 fluid ounce (2 tablespoons)	30 milliliters
1 cup (16 tablespoons)	240 milliliters
1 ounce (by weight)	28 grams
1 pound (16 oz)	454 grams
2.2 pounds	1 kilogram

Abbreviations

Measure	Abbreviation
Teaspoon	t or tsp
Tablespoon	T
Cup	c
Pound	lb
Ounce	oz
Fluid Ounce	fl oz
Gram	g
Kilogram	kg
Milliliter	mL

Index

*Page numbers in **bold** refer to recipes. Page numbers in *italics* refer to photos*

*Page numbers in **bold** refer to recipes. Page numbers in *italics* refer to photos*

*Page numbers in **bold** refer to recipes. Page numbers in *italics* refer to photos*

*Page numbers in **bold** refer to recipes. Page numbers in *italics* refer to photos*

*Page numbers in **bold** refer to recipes. Page numbers in *italics* refer to photos*

*Page numbers in **bold** refer to recipes. Page numbers in *italics* refer to photos*

Index   185

Made in the USA
Charleston, SC
25 September 2013